DAVID HUME
and the
History of England

Memoirs of the
AMERICAN PHILOSOPHICAL SOCIETY
Held at Philadelphia
For Promoting Useful Knowledge
Volume 131

DAVID HUME
and the
History of England

VICTOR G. WEXLER

Associate Professor of History
University of Maryland Baltimore County

THE AMERICAN PHILOSOPHICAL SOCIETY
Independence Square·Philadelphia

1979

Library of Congress Catalog Card Number 78-068423
International Standard Book Number 0-87169-131-0
US ISSN 0065-9738

To
My Mother
and in memory of
My Father

CONTENTS

Preface

This is a book about a man and a book. David Hume's
History of England was a very personal document. Because
prior to his beginning the *History* he had precious little success at making his philosophy known or understood, he
viewed the *History* as a last-ditch attempt to make himself
heard. Before the *History* appeared, he was for the most part
tucked away at Ninewells or in Edinburgh—which had not
yet become the "Athens of the North"—where he had little
money and virtually no recognition. He did experience some
luck with the sale of the first two volumes of his *Essays, Moral
and Political* in the early 1740's, but it was not enough to make
him what he wanted to be: an independent man of letters.
He needed that independence if only to end having to take
positions that either suited him poorly, such as that of a
merchant, or were humiliating, such as that of a tutor or
governor. He wanted to obtain a position at the universities
of Edinburgh and Glasgow but his relatively low birth and his
openly skeptical attitude toward Christianity made that impossible. He was a great man, and he knew it, but until 1754,
few listened to him.

Hume had no calling to be a historian. Relatively late in life
he tried the *metiér* and, after a short period of disappointment, finding that he could make it, he persevered, putting
everything into his historical career. The *History* evolved into
an extension of Hume's study of the "science of man;" conse-
quently I shall discuss some of the ways in which his politics,
moral values, and epistemology found their way into his
investigation of the past. I shall also discuss in chapter three
on Tudor history and the Scottish perspective, how the *History* became a polemical document in favor of the partisans of
progress in Scotland in the 1750's, those literati who wished
their country to become part of the mainstream of the European Enlightenment.

I approach the *History* as Hume did, dealing with it first as
the germ of a fertile idea and following that idea through ten

years of composition demonstrating where Hume personalized the past. I examine Hume's use of those who helped him arrive at his historical insights, but since he was relatively closed-mouthed about his sources, this process is somewhat speculative.

I also consider the rather unfortunate reputation of Hume as a historian and try to give him his due, because the *History* deserves it, after a long period of denigration, mostly, but not exclusively in the nineteenth century. Two books, one by Giuseppe Giarrizzo, *David Hume politico e storico* (Milan, 1962) and Duncan Forbes's *Hume's Philosophical Politics* (Cambridge, 1975) have long portions devoted to a fair and learned understanding of Hume as a historian, and I owe intellectual debts to both scholars, although they, of course, disagree. Giarrizzo is almost exclusively concerned with the relation between Hume's historical and political thought, emphasizing the turn toward conservatism that he believes the *History* shows. That turn, according to Giarrizzo, was prompted by the Jacobite uprising of 1745 and by Hume's general contempt for the new-moneyed England, the reliance on public financing, and the corrupt practices of the Whig government. Forbes, on the other hand, sees Hume's philosophy as unchanging, as that of the detached "philosophical" spectator commenting on the affairs and history of a country that was not his own. I believe that Hume's contribution can be understood without having to split his philosophy into distinct periods as Giarrizzo does, or without having to insist on Hume's impartiality as Forbes does. My debt to J. G. A. Pocock's classic study of *The Ancient Constitution and the Feudal Law: A Study of English Historical Thought in the Eighteenth Century* (New York, 1967), which provides the seventeenth-century background for Hume's assault on ancient constitutionalism, will be apparent in the final chapter.

My own approach is in part biographical and naturally I am indebted to Ernest C. Mossner's standard biography, *David Hume* (Austin, Texas, 1954), but I cannot accept his presentation of Hume as forever happy. To do that one has to take his short autobiography too literally. I wish to show how the *History of England* made Hume happy and thereby altered the course of his life. The reader will not find here an analysis of Hume either as a social historian or as a historian of religious ideas. Although Hume was interested in the new social history of the Enlightenment, he does not dwell on the development of culture as Voltaire attempted to do. His observations concerning the customs of the age serve as supplements to his narrative, but are in no way essential to his version of how the English constitution changed since the arrival of the Romans in Britain. Similarly, Hume failed to treat religion as a legitimate motive in influencing the course of English history, although he had to concede that, from time to time, it attributed to such momentous events as the seventeenth-century civil war. The Middle Ages were as dark to him as they were to Voltaire. He showed sympathy for victims of superstition, but paid only cursory attention to the role of religion and religious institutions. The emphasis of this study is on the biography of a book, how it originated and became the successful vehicle for its author's politics and world view.

Hume became a historian on the job; he had no systematic notion how to proceed: he went on because he liked the career of historian, and because he was good at it. But Hume's decision to become a historian not only changed his life, it also influenced British historiography; therefore, I assess how his acquired vocation affected the history of history. In the best tradition of the philosophes he was inspired by the need to criticize, but his criticism had a positive effect on the development of British historiography. Like the philosophes in general, he was quick to use the work of others to aid him in dispelling the myths that attended his particular area of interest. The Whigs had to suffer as a result of his critique, but their interpretation of English history has survived, and forms a permanent part of the English genius.

In the course of writing this book, I have accumulated a number of debts which I am pleased to acknowledge. My friend and teacher Peter Gay was a patient and helpful critic of several drafts, and my colleague, Robert K. Webb, became an insightful editor. My friends, Margaret Masson, Sandra Hebert, James Sturm, David Thaxton, Angela Wray, and Travis Clary all offered suggestions and encouragement. My greatest personal debt is to my parents. I only regret that my father, who was an inspiration throughout, did not live to see it come into print.

V. G. W.

Introduction: Hume Before the *History*

THE IMAGE of Hume as a jovial, benevolent, self-confident philosophe is one created mostly by a winsome little autobiography and the testimony of a few influential friends. *My Own Life* records Hume's frustrations, disappointments, and failures clearly enough, but the impression that prevails most readily lends itself to the traditional conception of Hume as the widely acclaimed man of letters whom the French called "le bon David." Hume's authoritative biographer describes in what sense his subject was known as good: "he was humane, charitable, pacific, tolerant, and encouraging of others, morally sincere and intellectually honest."[1] And it is true that Hume possessed all of these qualities—he is even able to convey them himself when he speaks of his indifference to his repeated but unsuccessful attempts to revise the *Treatise;* or when he describes himself as a man of "mild dispositions, of command of temper, of an open, social and cheerful humour, capable of attachment, but little susceptible of enmity, and of great moderation in all my passions."[2]

A few days after Hume's death, Joseph Black wrote to Adam Smith that even on his deathbed, Hume "never dropped the smallest expression of impatience but when he had occasion to speak to the people about him always did it with affection & tenderness,"[3] and William Cullen noted that as Hume approached death, "he constantly discovered a strong sensibility to the attention and care of his friends, and, amidst great uneasiness and languor, never betrayed any peevishness or impatience."[4] Adam Smith's panegyric is the document most responsible for the legends that abound concerning Hume's gentle character. "His temper," wrote Smith, "indeed seemed to be more happily balanced, if I may be

---

[1] Mossner, 1954: p. 4.
[2] Hume, 1882: **3:** pp. 7-8.
[3] Hume, 1932: **2:** p. 449.
[4] *Ibid.*, p. 450.

1

allowed such an expression, than that perhaps of any other man I have ever known. Even in the lowest state of his fortune, his great and necessary frugality never hindered him from exercising, upon proper occasions, acts both of charity and generosity."[5] While I have no intention of refuting most of the facts of Hume's autobiography or the admiring tributes of his friends, it should be stressed that Hume's life before he became a historian consisted mostly of personal isolation, smarting rejection, and humiliating circumstances. He may have been gracious and generous as an old man, but he could not have been so early in his life, even if he wished to: he was too poor and too insecure. None of his great works made him rich or well known until his *History of England* became a best seller.

My Own Life is the product of an accomplished intellectual who faced death bravely in part because the last twenty years of his life were fulfilling. But twenty years are not a lifetime, and retrospective reminiscence quite naturally softens the recollections of an unhappy youth, a distressing adolescence, and a frustrating middle age. The autobiography contains very few actual inaccuracies—it is the tone that is deceptive for the most part. Hume had a finely developed sense of decorum that was altogether in keeping with an Augustan style: there is much he does not talk about, and he probably thought it proper to glide over the rough spots, not only in the autobiography, but to a lesser extent in his letters to his closest friends as well. It is not out of a desire to deprive Hume of his privacy that I wish to examine his account of his life with an eye focused to recognize his moments of anguish: it is the desire to understand more fully the relationship between an author and the book that dramatically changed his life that has prompted the present study, especially because both the author and the book had a great impact on the age of Enlightenment. Undertaking the *History of England* was a turning point in Hume's life, and since this study is devoted to how Hume's decision to become a historian affected his subsequent life as well as the development of British historical thought, some attention needs to be paid here to Hume's life prior to the time he started to write the one book that gave him the recognition he hoped all his works would bring.

---

[5] *Ibid.*, p. 452.

What little we know about Hume's childhood does not suggest that it was very happy. His father died when he was only two years old. The family was not rich and most of what was to be inherited was of course left to his older brother: Hume's preoccupation with financial independence can surely be traced to the realization that he would have to strike out on his own. Although there is no evidence that shows the Humes of Ninewells to have been exceptionally religious, they, by law, had to attend church regularly and observe the infamous Scottish Sabbath, and Hume grew to loathe the gloomy brand of Calvinism that had been imported into Scotland; we shall see in our examination of the Tudor volumes of his *History*, how he demonstrated that contempt as an adult. As a youth Hume was isolated by his exceptional intelligence; his career as a student in Edinburgh was merely a formal ritual: he was for the most part an autodidact. He turned to books for company as well as for the wisdom and morality of the ancients.

The main document that discusses Hume's formative years is a letter to the rather well-known Scots physician and man of letters, Dr. George Cheyne. It is a striking piece, one which Hume surely wanted destroyed with the rest of his personal correspondence.[6] Hume felt he could trust Cheyne because of Cheyne's interest in literature as well as his medical expertise; indeed, Cheyne's affinity for books made him more accessible to Hume than any physician closer at hand. Hume wrote of his "Inclination to Books and Letters" that started in boyhood and flourished quite independently of his brief stay at the University of Edinburgh. At eighteen, he tells Cheyne, he experienced an emotional conversion when he abandoned the study of law, which he had been "designed to follow" but which appeared "nauseous" to him, in favor of a career of a "Scholar and Philosopher." After pursuing his philosophical studies for nine months he became seriously depressed: "all my Ardor seem'd in a moment to be extinguished." His symptoms included "scurvy spots" on the fingers and "Ptyalism or Watryness in the mouth." He consulted a physician at the time who treated the symptoms as hysterical, and told him that he had contracted the "Disease of the Learned." Hume took "Bitters and Anti-hysteric Pills" and within a year's time, he felt normal. What passed into his

---

[6] *Ibid.* **1:** p. xxi.

adult life from this adolescent crisis was an extraordinary
emotional investment in the success of his writings. He cured
himself of his melancholia by pouring himself into his work,
and although he decided to try the active life for a while as a
merchant in Bristol, he realized that his future lay some-
where in the Republic of Letters. He was quite apprehensive
that he would fail: "I had no hopes of delivering my Opinions with such Elegance & Neatness, as to draw to me the
Attention of the World & I wou'd rather live & dye in
Obscurity than produce them maim'd & imperfect." His
struggle for literary success was made all the more arduous
because of his "bashful Temper" and "narrow fortune."[7]

   After a few months in Bristol, Hume left for France in the
winter of 1734. Unfortunately no letters exist for the period
he spent at La Flèche (1734-1737), when, in virtual seclusion,
he composed *The Treatise of Human Nature* which he hoped
would "produce almost a total Alteration in Philosophy."[8] He
then spent two years in London polishing the work he also
hoped would end his isolation and relative poverty. But the
applause he was waiting for never reached him. Even though
the work had been published by a respectable house, it was
almost totally ignored. He returned to Ninewells in the
summer of 1739 a defeated man. Although *My Own Life*
acknowledges the failure, Hume makes it appear less painful
than I believe it was. In what has become a classic phrase, he
wrote that the *Treatise* "fell deadborn from the press." "But,"
he quickly added, "being naturally of a cheerful and san-
guine Temper, I very soon recovered the Blow, and prose-
cuted with great Ardour my Studies in the Country."[9] Hume
was somewhat less guarded in his correspondence. Two
weeks after publication Hume wrote to Henry Home (later
Lord Kames), who would be a lifelong friend, of his concern
about the reception of his creation: "You'll excuse the
natural Frailty of an Author in writing so long a Letter about
nothing but his own Performances. Authors have this Privilege in common with Lovers, & founded on the same Reason,
that they are both besotted with a blind Fondness of their
Object."[10] Hume here began to personify his works; this type

---

[7] *Ibid.*, pp. 12-18.
[8] Hume, 1954: p. 3.
[9] Hume, 1882: **3**: p. 2.
[10] Hume, 1954: p. 4.

of intense personal relationship between the creator and the created object continued sporadically for the rest of his life. Once back in Scotland he again wrote to Home that because of the "Success of my Philosophy. . . I am now out of Humour with myself; but doubt not in a little time to be only out of Humour with the World, like other unsuccessful Authors."[11] Although he soon began to work on his *Essays, Moral and Political* (Vol. 1, 1741, Vol. II, 1742), he hardly mentioned these works in his letters. He says in *My Own Life* that the essays were well received and "made me entirely forget my former Disappointment,"[12] but in his letters, he is constantly preoccupied with the necessity of finding an income.

Whatever success the *Essays* enjoyed, Hume never became as absorbed in writing them as he had been in *Treatise;* moreover, they did not obviate the need to apply for work as a governor or as a tutor. It was with humility bordering on self-effacement that the author of the *Treatise* had to ask an influential friend of the family to recommend him for a post as governor to the children of Lord Haddington.[13] When, in 1744, he was turned down for the chair in philosophy at Edinburgh, he had to consider instead a position as traveling tutor to the son of Lord Murray of Broughton.[14]

The position he finally found turned out to be the most miserable of all the possibilities. In 1745 Hume became the tutor to the mad Marquess of Annandale in London. *My Own Life* matter-of-factly states that Hume spent a year in that household and that as a result he made a "considerable accession to my small fortune."[15] On closer examination, the situation seems to have been considerably more frustrating and embarrassing. As the year progressed so did the insanity of the Marquess, and Hume had to do the work of a nurse; moreover, Captain Philip Vincent, who had engaged Hume, and was in charge of the Annandale estate at the time, appeared more and more unscrupulous and condescending. After one year Hume decided he had had enough. Vincent

---

[11] *Ibid.*, p. 5. Only Book I, "Of the Understanding," and Book II "Of the Passions," were published in 1739 by John Noon. In November, 1740, Thomas Longman published Book III, "Of Morals."

[12] Hume, 1882: **3:** p. 6.

[13] Hume, 1932: **1:** p. 36.

[14] *Ibid.*, p. 57.

[15] Hume, 1882: **3:** p. 3.

did not want him to leave and refused to pay part of the promised salary. The whole incident embittered Hume enough that by 1761, when he no longer needed the money, he was still involved in a lawsuit to retrieve it. At that time he wrote to one of the executors of the Annandale estate that the unfortunate transactions of 1745 were "as fresh in my memory, as if they past yesterday."[16] The memory of that year was no doubt made even more painful by the death of his mother, whom he always referred to with affection.

The period from 1746 to 1748 was the only one in Hume's adult life when he did not attempt a new major literary undertaking. He was a private secretary to General St. Clair, whom he accompanied in an expedition to Brittany in 1747 and then on military missions to the courts of Vienna and Turin in 1748. Although he said in *My Own Life* that he spent these years "agreeably and in good company,"[17] and, although his letters to his brother describing his travels are cheerful enough, he nonetheless felt wrenched from his real vocation. Early in 1747 he mused out loud to Henry Home about what he was doing in the employ of a general; "to what can all this serve?" He spoke also of his uncertainty about receiving the proper pay, an understandable concern since it was for the money that he was forced into the position.[18] When he was on his way to Turin in the winter of 1748 he again made a candid observation to Home: "Everybody congratulates me upon the pleasure I am to reap from this jaunt: and really I have little to oppose to this prepossession, except an inward reluctance to leave my books, and leisure and retreat."[19] Toward the end of 1748 Hume decided to rework and republish the first book of the *Treatise,* but the *Enquiry Concerning Human Understanding,* as the work was eventually called, met with no more success than the *Treatise.* A new edition of his *Essays, Moral and Political* of the same year was also a failure.

In 1749 he returned to Ninewells to live with his brother—there was nowhere else to go. He wrote in *My Own Life* that his "disappointments made little or no Impression

---

[16] Hume, 1932: **1:** p. 337.
[17] Hume, 1882: **3:** p. 3.
[18] Hume, 1932: **1:** p. 99.
[19] *Ibid.,* p. iii.

on me."[20] But his assessment of the progress of his life to his friend Home conveyed a sense of controlled despair:

> On the one hand, I consider, that I am at a critical Season in Life; & that if I retire into a Solitude at present I am in danger of being left there, & of continuing a poor Philosopher for ever. On the other hand, I am not able to form any distinct Project of pushing myself in any particular Profession; the Law & Army is too late, the Church is my Aversion. A traveling Tutor, some better, but not agreeable. Any Office uncertain, & precarious. Mean-while I lose my time, spend my Money; fall into necessity, perhaps, & Dependance, which I have sought all my Life to avoid. I am not a good Courtier, nor very capable of pushing my Fortune by Intrigue or Institution.[21]

Despite some improvement in the sales of *Essays* in 1750, and the successful appearance of his *Political Discourses* in 1752, Hume's life still appears, as he described it to Home, to have been one of wandering and failure. That sense of failure even crept into the carefully worded autobiography when he referred to the 1752 publication of a recasting of the third book of the *Treatise, An Enquiry Concerning the Principles of Morals.* He believed this to be the best of all his works yet "it came unnoticed and unobserved into the world."[22] His spirits were surely not improved by his second unsuccessful bid at entering the academic establishment; in the autumn of 1751 he was turned down for a position as professor of logic at Glasgow.

In 1752 Hume was forty-one years old. His principal source of pleasure in life came from studying and writing, yet his most important writings were ignored. He was uncomfortable in the active life because his heart was not in it. He had been humiliated and cheated at the household of a fabulously wealthy noble family in London, and even his claim for half-pay from the army due him from General St. Clair had been denied. There was no room for him at the universities of his native Scotland, and London appeared altogether hostile to an awkward, overweight philosopher with a Scots accent. He had some good friends like Adam Smith who knew how brilliant he was, and he himself dem-

---

[20] Hume, 1882: **3:** p. 3.
[21] Hume, 1952: **1:** pp. 25-26.
[22] Hume, 1882: **3:** p. 4.

onstrated remarkable pluck, considering the uphill battles he fought to be understood and accepted.

Hume finally received official recognition in February, 1752, when he was elected Keeper of the Library of the Faculty of Advocates in Edinburgh. He was of course pleased with the appointment, and a little surprised—the usual cabal had "entered into a regular concert" against him as they did when he was considered for the position at the university, but this time, despite "the violent cry of Deism, atheism and scepticism,"[23] he won. The salary was not great but the opportunities were. He really had no idea that before the year was over he would be launched on the most rewarding intellectual adventure of his life, the *History of England*. All he knew was that he now had a chance to pursue a new career. There was a lot riding on the future of his *History*, for, despite his official aloofness to criticism as recorded in his autobiography, Hume was "trembling" about the reception of the first volume of the *History* when it was ready for publication.[24] Had the *History* failed, even the "bon David" might not have been able to preserve his outward joviality.

John Stuart Mill once called Hume the "profoundest negative thinker upon record"[25] and this study of Hume and the *History* will in some sense vindicate that remark. Hume pursued the *History* with vigor in part because he found it to be an effective vehicle for criticizing the Whigs whom he believed held a stranglehold on places, positions, and literary taste. He hated them because they monopolized a world where he could, in fact, find no satisfactory place and because they could, to use his phrase, "purchase" the truth.[26] What effect Hume's assault had on the Whig interpretation and on British historiography—the ways in which he departed from tradition and influenced subsequent historians—is part of the same story of how Hume's becoming a historian gave a new direction to his life, and expanded his career as a philosophe.

---

[23] Hume, 1932: **1**: p. 165.
[24] *Ibid.*, p. 193.
[25] Mill, 1962: p. 88.
[26] "A Whig, who can give hundreds a year, will not be contented with small sacrifices of truth, and most authors are willing to purchase favour at so reasonable a price." Hume, 1932: **1**: p. 214.

I. The Early Stuarts: A "New Scene" of Historical Thought

M y *Own Life* is misleading about Hume's debut as a historian. Hume gave the impression that he proceeded directly and methodically from the writing of philosophy and literary and political essays to the writing of history, trying each genre in its turn, in order to be as inclusive as possible in his observations of human behavior, and also trying to reach a wider audience with each effort. He also maintained that it was not until his election as Keeper of the Library of the Faculty of Advocates in Edinburgh, in 1752, that he "formed the plan of writing the *History of England.*"[1]

Yet Hume first began to think about writing history at an earlier date. Between the publication of the *Treatise* in 1739 and his election to the post at the Library, Hume wrote several essays that were actually excursions into historical writing. "Of the Rise and Progress of the Arts and Sciences" (1742) and "Of the Populousness of Ancient Nations" (1751), two of Hume's arguments in behalf of cosmopolitan culture and modern civilization, are based on historical observation. Even the rather shallow essay "Of the Study of History" (1742), which he later termed "frivolous" and deleted from all editions of his works after 1746, gives evidence that he was concerned with history as a genre, before the 1750's.

In 1747 Hume had expressed the desire for more leisure time and for an income that would permit him "to prosecute my historical projects."[2] These historical projects probably refer to the memorandum for the *History of England,* written as early as 1745, during the miserable year he spent in London as a tutor to Annandale. Four of Hume's memoranda for the *History of England* are extant, and in two respects they belie the oversimplified account of the *History* as related in *My Own Life.*

---

[1] Hume, 1882: **3**: p. 4.
[2] Hume, 1932: **1**: p. 99.

First, the manuscripts—although not in Hume's handwriting—are signed and inscribed by him with dates prior to his election as Keeper of the Library of the Faculty of Advocates.[3] Second, these chronological outlines for the history of England range from the Roman invasion of Britain to the reign of George II. That Hume had sketched England's history from antiquity as early as 1745 means that, despite his assertion in *My Own Life,* he did not initially plan to begin the *History* with "the accession of the House of Stuart, an epoch when, I thought, the misrepresentation of faction began chiefly to take place."[4]

This much of his autobiographical account is accurate: not until 1752 did he begin to do sustained work on the history he projected. Hume's election as keeper in January, 1752, was cause for celebration among his friends, and he was gratified by public recognition in the city where, in 1745, he had been denied the chair of moral philosophy.[5] Provided with the surroundings and the books he needed, Hume began in earnest to execute those "historical projects" which already existed in outline form.

Something more than his position at the Library with its 30,000-volume collection was necessary, however, to transform his inchoate historical interests and his notes into a coherent literary reality. Hume had to find his place in the writing of English history, through his own interpretation, just as he had found it in the writing of philosophy. Once he had detected where the commonplace notions of English historiography could be challenged, he would know where to begin his own history, and how to render the work of his predecessors obsolete. Like other philosophes, he had to destroy in order to build. He needed, in short, to open up "a new Scene of Thought," as he did at the age of eighteen when, "transported beyond measure" he renounced the study of law in favor of philosophy and literature.[6]

There is evidence that Hume experienced a similar intellectual awakening at the time he formally began the *History of*

---

[3] These manuscripts are listed as *Historical Memoranda* in the bibliography; attention was first brought to them by Mossner, 1941.

[4] Hume, 1882: **3:** p. 4.

[5] The full account of the charges brought against Hume in 1745, as well as his reply to them, is available in Hume, 1967.

[6] Hume, 1932: **1:** p. 1.

England. The evidence dates from 1752, the time of the election to the keepership, to 1754, when the first volume of the *History* was published; it indicates the nature of Hume's new interpretation as well as his reasons for beginning his narrative with the accession of the Stuarts, rather than with the Romans, as his early sketches had indicated. The crucial new insight concerned events in the seventeenth century; the first sign emerges in a letter to Adam Smith, dated eight months after he had assumed his responsibilities at the Library. Hume wrote with obvious excitement:

> 'Twas under James that the House of Commons began first to raise their Head, & then the Quarrel betwixt Privilege and Prerogative commenc'd. The Government no longer opprest by the enormous Authority of the Crown displayed its Genius; and the Factions, which then arose, having an Influence on our present Affairs, form the most curious, interesting, and instructive Part of our History. . . . I confess, that the Subject appears to me very fine; and I enter upon it with great Ardour and Pleasure. You need not doubt my Perseverance.[7]

From this moment on, his letters are permeated with the contentment of a scholar who had at last found his vocation.

By January, 1753, Hume had finished the reign of James I; and by May of the same year he was able to inform Smith that he was beginning the Long Parliament. "Were you not my Friend," he wrote in his most cheerful letter to date, "you wou'd envy my robust Constitution. My Application has been and is continual, and yet I preserve entire health."[8] Hume did more than persevere following the publication of the first volume of the *History,* which he personified as "my youngest and dearest child"[9] in October, 1754; he was eagerly applying a discovery he thought would vitiate the standard Whig interpretation of seventeenth-century English history.

In the eighteenth century, Whig historians tended to interpret the seventeenth century in much the same way as the parliamentary opponents of the Stuarts had described their own program. They presented the battle between the king and Parliament as one of royal usurpation of ancient liberties versus legal, parliamentary resistance to despotic

---

[7] Hume, 1932: **1:** p. 168.
[8] *Ibid.,* p. 176.
[9] *Ibid.,* p. 196.

designs. Since the Glorious Revolution of 1688, and the consequent Whig supremacy, party propaganda had been presented as an accurate account of what had actually occurred during almost a century of parliamentary conflict with the Stuart monarchs. These historians seldom adhered to the Whig formula as rigidly as Hume claimed; he overemphasized the deficiencies typical of Whig history, and, as a result, drew something of a caricature of it. But in reacting to them he was able to create what he occasionally insisted was the first truly impartial history of England. By arguing that the House of Commons, not the king, was the aggressor, Hume arrive at (to adapt his own phrase) a new scene of historical thought. He believed that he could now proceed to dispel historical myths just as he had previously challenged the accepted premises of rationalist philosophy. The philosophe had glimpsed the place where he might be as skeptical in history as he had been in philosophy.

At this point in his career as a historian he did not realize that he was about to open once more the seventeenth-century historiographical controversy concerning the ancient constitution and antiquity of the Commons. Nor does he seem to have been aware that in the 1730's there had been a temporary reversal of the Whig and Tory positions concerning the history of the constitution. Walpole's propagandists at that time were forced to adopt some Tory-sounding historical principles in government-sponsored newspapers, in order to defend the ministry against Bolingbroke's charges of despotism. By the time he completed the task of writing the *History*, however—moving backwards in time through the Middle Ages—he had become fully aware that he had placed himself in the tradition of the seventeenth-century critics (principally Sir Robert Brady) who denied that the Commons held their rights from time immemorial. But in the 1750's, having read the formal historical works that outlived Walpole and the vagaries of Augustan political pamphleteering,[10] Hume confined himself to refuting what continued to be the prevailing eighteenth-century version of the Whig interpretation of early Stuart history.

---

[10] The sinuous contours of this pamphlet war are carefully sorted out by Isaac Kramnick, 1967: **6**: pp. 35-67. Kramnick extended his argument in *Bolingbroke and His Circle: The Politics of Nostalgia in the Age of Walpole* (Cambridge, 1968), especially Chapter VI, "Bolingbroke on Politics and the English Constitution," pp. 137-138.

Hume chose Paul de Rapin-Thoyras as his Whig foil. Rapin was a French Protestant refugee who had fled to England after the revocation of the Edict of Nantes. Finding no position in the academies or the court dominated by a Catholic English king, he fled again to Holland. In 1688 he returned to England in the entourage of William of Orange. In 1700 King William III granted him a pension, and Rapin began his multi-volume *Histoire d'Angleterre,* which appeared between 1723 and 1725.[11] Rapin's work, immediately translated into English by Nicholas Tindal, who, as expected, called it "the most impartial History of England yet extant,"[12] was the most widely read English history written in the eighteenth century—until Hume's.

Indebted as he obviously was to the establishment of a limited and Protestant monarchy in England, Rapin was naturally inclined to be sympathetic to the parliamentary cause. In an effort to convince readers of the impartiality of the history he was now beginning to write, Hume exaggerated Rapin's partiality. Yet, before realizing that he might discredit the typical Whig view in his own *History,* he considered Rapin a perfectly satisfactory historian. In his essay "Of the Protestant Succession," written in 1748, but withheld from publication until 1752, Hume calls Rapin "the most judicious of historians";[13] however, in the edition of the essay ready for publication in 1753, a few months before the publication of the first volume of the *History of England,* he denounced Rapin as a historian who, "suitable to his usual malignity and partiality," treats the Stuarts with "too much severity."[14] This change was indeed important, as Hume explained in a letter written in 1757 to the Abbé Le Blanc, who was editing and translating the essays for a French edition: "To tell the Truth, I was carry'd away with the usual Esteem pay'd to that Historian, till I came to examine him more particularly when I found him altogether despicable; & I was not asham'd to acknowledge my Mistake."[15]

In 1752 and 1753, during the composition of the first volume of the *History,* Hume's letters document his disillu-

---

[11] Firth, 1896: **16:** pp. 740-743.
[12] Rapin, 1738: **3:** p. iii.
[13] Hume, 1882: **3:** p. 473n.
[14] *Ibid.*
[15] Hume, 1932: **1:** p. 258.

sionment with Rapin. In January, 1753, after completing the reign of James I, he was confident enough to declare to Clephane, "You know that there is no post of honour in the English Parnassus more vacant than that of History. Style, judgement, impartiality, care—everything is wanting to our historians; and even Rapin, during this latter period [the seventeenth century] is extremely deficient."[16] Six months later, the grudging "even" was gone, and a more audacious Hume, increasingly hopeful that his *History* would enjoy the success that the *Treatise* had deserved but failed to achieve, wrote:

> The more I advance in my undertaking, the more am I convinced that the History of England has never yet been written, not only for style, which is notorious to all the world, but also for matter; such is the ignorance and partiality of all our historians. Rapin, whom I have esteem for, is totally despicable.[17]

Hume was preparing his friends for his "youngest and dearest child": he was intimating to them his aim of replacing Rapin as the popular historian of Great Britain; he even indicated where his "impartiality" and originality lay, and why Rapin should be dismissed as a party historian. In order to evaluate Hume's claims for his history of the early Stuarts, it is necessary to take a look at this volume.

In Hume's first volume (which in 1754 bore the title *The History of Great Britain*), James I appeared as a victim of forces beyond his control and comprehension. Hume was sympathetic to a Stuart king who was as much a foreigner in London as Hume had been when he traveled south to the capital, but Hume's generous portrait of James does not arise out of an affinity for a fellow Scot. It is a product of his perception that the aggressiveness of the leaders of the Commons was unprecedented in the history of the English constitution. According to Hume, for three centuries before the accession of James, regal authority—the dispensing power, the power of imprisonment, the exacting of loans and

---

[16] *Ibid.*, p. 170.

[17] *Ibid.*, p. 179. Duncan Forbes notes Hume's disenchantment with Rapin in his "Introduction" to a reprinting of *The History of Great Britain* (Baltimore, 1970), p. 29. It is one of my objectives here to answer as much as possible Forbes's implicit request for documentation concerning "when and why" Hume came to write history, a task Giarrizzo believed "futile." p. 129.

benevolences, the right to alter customs duties or sell monopolies— had never been questioned. The first Stuart provoked the Commons with his speeches on divine right but his haughty pronouncements were necessitated, Hume thought, "by reason of the opposite doctrines, which *began* to be promulgated by the puritanical party" in the Commons.[18]

To Rapin, James had appeared a belligerent, plotting prince bent on establishing despotic power.[19] A precise instance where Hume and Rapin disagreed can be seen in their presentation of the king's interference with the free election of members to the Commons. Hume maintained that the king was executing a traditionally accepted royal prerogative. James's actions may have been unwise; nevertheless, Hume presented them as the practice of earlier times and of his own: "In former periods of the English government the house of commons was of so small a weight in the balance of the constitution that little attention has been given, either by the crown, the people of the house itself, to the choice and continuance of the members."[20] Rapin simply contended that such interference was unprecedented.[21]

Hume did more than disagree with Rapin. Hume continually refined and reinforced his argument in subsequent editions by adding to and deleting from earlier editions. His position on the king's right to levy impositions is a case in point.

In the first version of his defense of James, the 1754 *History of Great Britain,* Hume was fairly cautious about his case: "precedents were neither very recent nor very numerous. One in the reign of Mary, another in the beginning of

---

[18] Hume, 1778: **6:** p. 161. Hume's italics. All my references will be to this edition, which was the first to appear encompassing "the author's last corrections and improvements." It was reprinted several times in the last two decades of the eighteenth century by William Strahan, and his successor, T. Cadell; it is reasonably accessible both in Great Britain and in the United States. I have collated this first complete edition with the earlier ones published in Hume's lifetime, which are available at the British Museum Library and at the National Library of Scotland. Page references to the earlier editions will be noted when the passage cited cannot be found in the 1978 edition. Many of the abridged, expurgated editions of the *History* printed in the nineteenth century are, of course, untrustworthy. Some of the changes Hume made in the various editions are important indications of his everincreasing disdain for the Whig interpretation, an attitude he refined as he pursued his researches.

[19] Rapin, 1726-1731: **9:** p. 447.

[20] Hume, 1778: **6:** p. 15.

[21] Rapin, 1726-1731: **9:** p. 252.

Elizabeth, were the latest that could be found."[22] At the first
opportunity of rewriting, in 1759, he omitted this part of the
text, and wrote instead that the king "was supported in that
act of power by direct precedents, some from the reign of
Mary, some in the beginning of Elizabeth."[23] In 1762, when
the *History of England* appeared in its entirety for the first
time, he added a new comment on the resistance offered by
the Commons to time-honored royal prerogative:

> A spirit of liberty had now taken possession of the house: The
> leading members, men of an independent genius and large
> views, began to regulate their opinions, more by the future
> consequences which they foresaw, than by the former prece-
> dents which were set before them; and they less aspired at
> maintaining the ancient constitution, than at establishing a new
> one, and a freer, and a better.[24]

Having completed the *History,* Hume was all the more convinced that he had cast the roles of the protagonists correctly.
In this instance, moreover, he was certain enough of his case
to shift his argument from a defense of the crown's prescriptive claims to an attack on the innovations of the Commons.

In Hume's account of Charles's confrontations with the
Commons, he again differs from Rapin. Rapin has Charles
"designing" his financial problems in such a way as to call
upon the Commons in the atmosphere of an emergency. As
soon as the king had his money, his plan was to dismiss that
body "without going on to any other business."[25] Hume
attributed no such intentions to Charles. On the contrary, if a
deliberate plan was present in these encounters, Hume believed that it rested with the parliamentary opposition, with
its "intractable and encroaching spirit."[26]

Again in support of Charles, Hume deleted from his text,
just as he had done in behalf of James. Critical though he was
of Charles's support of Buckingham and of his war policy,
Hume became less critical when he realized that condemnation of the king's actions might attenuate the force of his
general defense of Charles. It was only in the first edition of
the *History of Great Britain* that he wrote:

---

[22] Hume, 1754, p. 35.
[23] Hume, 1778: **6:** p. 51.
[24] *Ibid.*
[25] Rapin, 1726-1731: **10:** p. 5.
[26] Hume, 1778: p. 391.

And to what purpose all these mighty stretches of prerogative, which tore and disjointed the whole fabric of the government and exhausted all the force of authority? Only to support Buckingham, a very unfit minister during such critical times; and to carry on a war with Spain; a war, in every respect unjust, unnecessary, and not recommended by the least success.[27]

This is the strongest criticism Hume ever made of Charles I. No matter how justified Hume thought he was initially, he preferred to drop his little diatribe, rather than disrupt the flow of the narrative or diminish the intellectual impact of the whole first volume of the *History*.

Hume set himself many goals in becoming a historian. One of them was to provide the British audience with a readable narrative history, the type of work it simply did not have in the eighteenth century. Rapin's many volumes are composed largely of reproductions of parliamentary speeches, interspersed with comments by the historian. By comparison, Hume's *History* is both economical and eloquent. He deliberately placed any lengthy digressions into footnotes, and his own gift for the carefully balanced sentences and subtle ironies that graced the finest neoclassical prose makes his *History* infinitely more attractive than the heavy sentences of Tindal's translation of a foreign work.

It was also important to Hume to be original. The perception that he could be original was, as we have seen, indispensable to his undertaking the *History*. But new interpretations almost always have their precedents—they are adumbrated in some form, even if the historian is unfamiliar with the origin of ideas he believes are all his own. What were Hume's? Unfortunately, they do not emerge as clearly in his history as in his philosophy. In the *Treatise*, Hume names Locke, Shaftesbury, Mandeville, Butler, and Hutcheson as having "put the science of man on a new footing."[28] In addition to Hume's statement naming his philosophical forebears, we have his early drafts of parts of the *Treatise*.[29] The only overt expression of gratitude Hume ever made concerning the construction of the first volume of the *History* was to Clarendon.

---

[27] Hume, 1754: p. 163.
[28] Hume, 1882: p. 308.
[29] Hume, 1932: 1: pp. 33, 39.

He acknowledged Clarendon as the principal source for his description of Charles's trial and execution; and his rhetorical debt to Clarendon for the moving account of the king's last days was great.[30] On the other hand, so was the difference with which Hume viewed Charles's demise and the dissolution of the monarchy. To Clarendon, the regicide was a heinous, atheistical crime against a "saint-like, blessed monarch," an "unparalleled murder and parricide," which had to be atoned for in a "blessed restoration."[31] It has been well observed that Clarendon saw the Restoration as a "divine attestation of the English Church," a miracle, which "stood on a level with the dryshod passage of the Israelites through the Red Sea."[32] Hume wrote without Clarendon's sentimentality and without Clarendon's reverence for the Church: his sympathy for Charles at the end of the first volume of the *History of Great Britain* was based on the insistence that the revolution which ended in regicide began gradually as the Commons first began their assault during the reign of James I. In addition, Clarendon began his narrative with the Long Parliament, and conceived of the Civil War more in terms of a religious conflict, personified in the leaders on all sides. Hume's aim was to deal with the evolution of the constitution from the accession of James, offering, as he saw it, a challenging interpretation of the history of the early Stuarts. We can only guess which historians helped Hume to his conclusions.

Ironically, traces of Hume's interpretations can be found in the works of the very historians he was determined to discredit. In the history of the "despicable" Rapin, and even more in the work of Laurence Echard, whose *History of England* (1707) was the standard history in the eighteenth century until Tindal's translation of Rapin appeared, the stage is vaguely set for Hume. True, Rapin insisted that Charles I systematically planned "to carry the regal authority to much greater lengths than had his father or any of his predecessors,"[33] and that both during the Parliament of 1640 and before, the king had "subverted the constitution."[34] Yet

---

[30] Hume, 1778: **7**: p. 108.
[31] Clarendon, 1888: pp. 484-511.
[32] Wormald, 1964: p. 239.
[33] Rapin, 1726-1731: **10**: p. 3.
[34] *Ibid.*, p. 22.

Rapin was aware of the pitfalls of party history and even delineates its extremes, maintaining of course that he supported neither side. Rapin did have his bias and Hume disagreed with it, but he was hardly the dogged Whig that Hume denounced. His sensitivity to both the royalist and parliamentarian "scheme" of history may well have stimulated Hume to his own version of the conflict.[35]

Nor does Echard's work coincide with what Hume would have us believe all popular eighteenth-century historians wrote of the seventeenth century. Despite his hyperbolic celebration of the Glorious Revolution as the "most wonderful and providential" event that every happened, Echard is quite fair-minded in describing the uncertain state of "the liberties of the people" during the reigns of the first two Stuarts.[36] Indeed, Echard was bitterly criticized by the Reverend Edmund Calamy for not following the Whig Canon. Calamy, who wrote that the reign of Charles I represented "one continual invasion upon the rights of the people,"[37] fits very well into Hume's formula of the Whig interpretation, but there were some historians from whom Hume may have learned more than he would have cared to admit.

To be sure, Hume was not the first in the eighteenth century to criticize Rapin's history of the seventeenth century, or the Whig notion of an ancient constitution. Walpole's hacks saw to that as part of their reply to Bolingbroke, as did the well-placed Lord Hervey in his *Ancient and Modern Liberty Stated and Compared* (1734). Hume was the first, however, to make this criticism of what he believed was a mythical view of the English constitution in a systematic manner, weaving a comprehensive historical narrative around a passionately perceived point of view. Walpole's press may have "broken the ground,"[38] but Hume alone was responsible for Rapin's decline in popularity and intellectual credibility. Moreover, Hume, more than any enlightened Whig, was able to carry his argument to its logical conclusion, maintaining that at least in the legal sense, the first Stuart kings were in the right.

---

[35] *Ibid.*, p. 14.

[36] Echard, 1718: **2**: p. 2.

[37] Calamy, 1718: p. 26. Elsewhere, Calamy wrote to Echard that "in the dedication of your second volume, and preface to the third, you applaud the Revolution. And in the history that follows, you as zealously applaud the principles that would have effectively prevented it." *Ibid.*, p. 22.

[38] Kramnick, 1967: p. 54.

It is possible that Hume arrived at his interpretation on the basis of primary evidence. In 1752, soon after assuming office as Keeper of the Library of the Faculty of Advocates, Hume ordered ten volumes of the *Journal of the House of Commons*, as well as several other collections of state papers, from Gavin Hamilton, the Edinburgh bookseller.[39] In the first two editions of the *History of Great Britain*, Hume did not cite them because, as he later explained to Horace Walpole, he had desired to follow the style of the best of the "modern historians," such as Machiavelli and Sarpi, who did not acknowledge their sources.[40]

Although in subsequent editions, Hume did cite some references, he never did so systematically; however, he did use both primary sources and secondary accounts in ways that we would consider acceptable today. He formed a hypothesis— one which did not appear as a whole in any of the sources— and then reinforced it with increased detail and conviction, incorporating the information as best he could. Whatever use he made of his predecessors, his formulation was singularly persuasive, and it had great impact on the reading public. He was the first (if not the last) historian to make the rise of the Commons the central issue in a fully developed constitutional history of England during the reigns of the early Stuarts.[41]

If Hume achieved his goal of originality in his first volume, what can be said of his claim to the quality that Voltaire chose to admire above all else in Hume's *History*, his impartiality, the greater objectivity of Hume when compared to Rapin.[42]

---

[39] "Register of the proceedings of the Curators and Keeper of the Library in relation to their Office Beginning Anno 1725." MS, National Library of Scotland. This particular sale is listed under the year 1752. In 1754, in one sale, Hume spent £ 50.12.12 at Gavin Hamilton's—more than his predecessor, Thomas Ruddiman, spent in an average year.

[40] Hume, 1932: 1: pp. 284-285. After Strahan had printed the first edition of Gibbon's *History*, with the references at the end of the volume, Hume suggested that the "authorities ought only to be printed at the Margin or the Bottom of the Page." Hume was "plagued" with the tedious process of turning to the end of the volume to check a reference. *Ibid.* 2: p. 313.

Perhaps another explanation for the omission of his references in the first two editions of the *History of Great Britain* lies in Hume's excessively negative reaction to Rapin, which was stylistic as well as intellectual. Rapin's bulky volumes are filled with reproductions of the parliamentary debates.

[41] Despite the inevitable revisions of more recent scholarship, Hume's interpretation, at least in kernel form, remains a classic. See, for example, Notestein, 1966.

[42] In May, 1764, Voltaire, in a review of Hume's *L'histoire complète de l'Angleterre* in *La Gazette Littéraire*, wrote that it was "perhaps the best ever written in any language.

If we judge either Hume or Voltaire by the standards of Ranke, or of our time, they will be found to be obviously tendentious. They conceived their works in polemical terms and consciously sought to make their politics evident—and all the more attractive—by writing with passion and humor. Hume did protest his neutrality, but as Leo Braudy has remarked, "faith in the possibility of his impartiality grows weaker as his claims of impartiality grow more shrill."[43] Moreover, it would be anachronistic, as Constant Noble Stockton reminds us, to confuse Hume's understanding of impartiality with what "recent methodologists have come to expect" from scientific history.[44] Hume was no more impartial than Voltaire.

Hume himself detected the conflict that existed in being both an open advocate of a particular interpretation and a disinterested recorder of events, and he hoped that he had made that conflict as acceptable to his contemporaries as it apparently was to him. Upon publication of his first volume, he wrote to his good friend, William Mure of Caldwell, "the first Quality of an Historian is to be true and impartial; the next is to be interesting. If you do not say, that I have done both Parties Justice; & if Mrs. Mure be not sorry for poor King Charles, I shall burn all my Papers, & return to Philosophy."[45] He never had to do that; in fact Hume's obvious and persuasive partiality accounts largely for the notoriety his *History* eventually achieved.

In assessing Hume's pretense of impartiality we can return to *My Own Life*, and his view of his position in the Whig-Tory debate:

> But though I had been taught by experience, that the Whig party were in possession of bestowing all places, both in the state and literature, I was so little inclined to yield to their

---

... Rapin Thoires, a foreigner, alone seemed to have written an impartial history; yet there is still the stain of prejudice on the truths that Thoires relates. In the new historian, instead of prejudice, we find a mind superior to his materials; he speaks of epidemic diseases." Voltaire, 1877-1885: **25:** pp. 169-173.

Like Hume, Voltaire at one time had thought that Rapin had written "the only good history of England." Voltaire, 1957: p. 1017.

[43] Braudy, 1970: p. 90. Hume himself gives up on the ghost of impartiality when he writes to his friend Gilbert Eliot of Minto that he really deserved the name of a "Party Writer." Hume, 1954: p. 70. The tone of this letter is ironic, but his confession of bias has the ring of simple truth.

[44] Stockton, 1971: p. 289. I cannot agree with Forbes, 1976: p. 219, that Hume was impartial in a philosophical and detached way.

[45] Hume, 1932: **1:** p. 210.

senseless clamour, that in about a hundred alterations, which
farther study, reading, or reflection engaged me to make in
the reigns of the first two Stuarts, I have made them all invari-
ably to the Tory side. It is ridiculous to consider the English
constitution before that period as a regular plan of liberty.[46]

I have indicated some of the substantial alterations; they
reveal that Hume had found his place in the history of
English historiography as an anti-Whig historian. He was
determined to replace Rapin, and he did. He confused his
readers by saying that he made his alterations to the Tory
side, rather than simply that he made them against the Whigs.
Hume often repeated that his second volume, containing the
reigns of Charles II and James II, showed him to be opposed
to a Tory interpretation of history. This was an unnecessary
insistence on his part; perhaps he made it because of the
criticism the first volume evoked, criticism that dismissed his
work as a mere panegyric of Charles I.[47] But his being an
anti-Whig in his first volume never meant that he was pro-
Tory.[48]

Samuel Johnson knew that Hume was no Whig, yet he did
not wish to admit him into a circle where he did not belong.
When Johnson condescendingly dubbed Hume "a Tory by
chance,"[49] he implied that Hume could never feel at home in
subscribing to the Tory's characteristic reverence for authority, monarchy, or religion. Hume's case for the first Stuarts
was historical, not sentimental. He had no use for their
religion or for their haughty conceptions of themselves as
divine-right monarchs. In the *History* itself he explains why
he came to their defense: "Though it must be confessed that
their skill in government was not proportioned to the ex-
treme delicacy of their situation; a sufficient indulgence has
not been given them and all the blame, by several historians,

---

[46] Hume, 1882: **3:** pp. 5-6.

[47] *The Monthly Review or Literary Journal* **12** (March, 1755): p. 229.

[48] I am in obvious disagreement with Professor Mossner, who concluded, on the
basis of a comparison of four different editions of Hume's first volume, that "Hume
far more closely approximated the ideal of philosophical indifferences or historical
impartiality than he seemed to give himself credit for in the notorious passage in *My
Own Life.*" Mossner, 1941: p. 233.

I think that Green, 1943: p. 334, did well to attribute some of Hume's apparent
sympathy for the Tory cause to his skeptical view of human nature and its inability
to challenge authority constructively, except under the most dire circumstances.

[49] Boswell, 1943-1950: **4:** p. 194.

has been unjustly thrown on *their* side."[50] Hume never en-
dorsed Tory principles. He had, in fact, formally denounced
them in his essay "Of Passive Obedience" (1748). That he
had discredited the principles of one party did not mean that
he had adopted the ideology of another.

The greatest goal Hume pursued as a historian was success. He readily confessed that this "love of literary fame"
was his "ruling passion,"[51] and he worked assiduously for
recognition as a man of letters, but without widespread
acclaim until he became a historian. Because the initial sale of
the first volume was small, Hume had reason to doubt the
effect of his interpretation when it was first published, but
those doubts must have faded by the mid-1760's, when
Catherine Graham Macaulay undertook a refutation of that
volume. Mrs. Macaulay explained that it was her intention to
restore dignity to the reputation of the parliamentary
leaders—a task made necessary by Hume's "unrivaled popularity in the walk of English history."[52] Mrs. Macaulay's republican verve made her *History* more readable than Rapin's,
but she followed Rapin in maintaining that the first two
Stuarts were despotic, arbitrary, and totally deserving of
their fate. Mrs. Macaulay's acclaim as a national historian was
second only to Hume's in the eighteenth century, and it is no
small compliment to him that she saw the need to revive and
revamp the Whig interpretation.

Hume was quite pleased to see Mrs. Macaulay's *History*,
and was not above using her researches to further his own
interpretation. In the 1770 edition of his *History*, Hume used
a letter Mrs. Macaulay had discovered in the British Museum
for a purpose opposed to the one for which she had cited it.
The letter in question, written by Charles to Henrietta Maria,
partially explains his affection for episcopacy: without control of an effective militia, he could use the bishops as a
means of retaining some authority in the kingdom. Hume
concluded that the letter demonstrated "the king's good
sense, and proves that his attachment to episcopacy, though
partly founded on religious principles, was also, in his situation, derived from the soundest of civil policy."[53] Hume's

---

[50] Hume, 1778: **6:** pp. 579-580. Hume's italics.
[51] Hume, 1882: **3:** p. 8.
[52] Catherine Graham Macaulay, 1763-1768: **6:** p. viii.
[53] Hume, 1778: **6:** p. 588.

use, in a new edition of his own work, of the letter she had
discovered must have infuriated Mrs. Macaulay. She had
maintained that the letter showed that a "passion for power
was Charles' predominant vice," and that his religious convic-
tions were insincere, "a secondary and subordinate affection."[54] This was only one of many instances where the two
historians disagreed. They viewed the entire history of the
seventeenth century in an antithetical manner. In a condescending letter thanking her for a complimentary copy of her
History Hume confessed that

> I have the misfortune to differ from you in some original
> principles. . . . I grant, that the cause of liberty, which you,
> Madam, with the Pyms and Hampdens have adopted, is noble
> and generous; but most of the partisans of that cause, in the
> last century disgraced it, by their violence, and also by their
> cant, hypocrisy, and bigotry, which, more than the principles
> of civil liberty, seem to have been the motive of all their actions.
> Had those principles always appaeared in the amiable light
> which they receive both from your person and writings, it
> would have been impossible to resist them; and however much
> inclined towards the first James, and Charles, I should have
> been the first to condemn those monarchs for not yielding to
> them.[55]

The force and confidence of Hume's letter reveal the deserved sense of accomplishment that he enjoyed as a result of
the first volume of his *History.* The fame he sought as a
philosopher and essayist he found as a historian.

Hume gained more than acclaim as a historian. He also
added a new dimension to his career as a philosophe. A
generation ago, Carl Becker wrote that Hume, alarmed by
the force of his skepticism, "turned away from speculation
to the study of history."[56] More recently, James Noxon
charged Hume with having foregone his original ambition of
an integrated science of man. To Noxon, Hume's metamor-
phosis from "experimental psychologist to philosophical historian" constituted a failure to realize a "comprehensive
philosophical system."[57] But Hume did not see it that way.

[54] Macaulay, 1763-1768: **4:** pp. 419-420.
[55] Hume, 1954: pp. 81-82.
[56] Carl Becker, 1932: p. 83.
[57] James Noxon, 1973: pp. 25-26. Not all critics have seen Hume's philosophical
and historical careers as dichotomous. Norton and Popkin convincingly argue that

The pleasure he took in showing that at least some Whigs had an enchanted view of English history is precisely the pleasure of a skeptical epistemologist, as he at the age of twenty-eight defined that term. Fools, he said in the *Treatise*, are the only ones who can believe in things with certainty, a "true sceptic will be diffident of his philosophical doubts."[58] The Whig historians tended to be too cocksure, but they were on the defensive after the appearance of Hume's *History;* in this respect Hume's historical debut had another ramification—Whigs through the nineteenth century, including Thomas Babington Macaulay, George Brodie, and Henry Hallam, had to grapple with Hume's challenge. Hume, of course, had no more way of knowing that, than of realizing the extent to which the *Treatise* would eventually influence the world of philosophy. Yet he did live long enough to know that the *History* had made an indelible mark on the evolution of British historiography. He was delighted to busy himself with his "youngest and dearest child" until the year of his death.

"history and philosophy are in Hume's thought inextricably bound together." Norton and Popkin, 1965: p. lx.

[58] Hume, 1882: 1: p. 552.

II. The Later Stuarts: Politics into History

DESPITE the excitement he felt at the prospect of a new career, Hume was depressed by the earliest reactions to the publication of his first volume. He received word from his bookseller in London that, in the twelve months immediately following the appearance of *The History of Great Britain,* only forty-five volumes had been sold. The perennial fear that his efforts would again be ignored disturbed him greatly. He was, he confessed, mortified by the thought that his book would "sink into oblivion."[1] In an attempt to improve sales and widen his audience, he decided to abandon the publisher of the first volume, Gavin Hamilton of Edinburgh, for Andrew Millar of London. It was a wise decision for two reasons: Millar was both a more efficient and aggressive businessman than Hamilton, and it was probably the case that publishers in London, hostile to competition from the north, blocked the sale of an Edinburgh publication.[2]

Second only to the pain of neglect was that the few readers who purchased Hume's first volume misunderstood the nature of his defense of the Stuarts. In addition to the broadside in the *Monthly Review* of March, 1755, which concentrated on the author's sardonic treatment of the religious conflicts of the 1640's, the Rev. William Warburton, accustomed to vilifying Hume as a skeptic, declared that his latest production showed him to be "an atheistical Jacobite, a monster as rare with us as a hippogriff."[3] Reflecting upon the reception of his first volume when he wrote the autobiography, Hume recorded his failure with a hint of the bitterness that he felt at the time. "I was assailed by one cry of reproach, disapprobation, and even detestation; English, Scotch, and Irish, Whig and Tory, churchman and sectary, freethinker and religionist, patriot and courtier, united in their rage against the man, who had presumed to shed a

---

[1] Hume, 1882: **3:** p. 5.
[2] Mossner and Ransom, 1950: pp. 162-182.
[3] Quoted in Mossner, 1954: p. 309.

26

generous tear for the fate of Charles I." With no small hint of irony Hume also recorded that the primates of England and Ireland were the only ones to send him "messages not to be discouraged."[4] The full extent of Hume's frustration is revealed in a letter written two months after the critique in the *Monthly Review* had appeared. Despite what he called his "Candor & Disinterestedness," he saw himself "torne in Pieces by Calumny. . . . I am dub'd a Jacobite, Passive Obedience Man, Papist & what not."[5]

Hume had the option of attenuating his case against the parliamentarians in order to mollify his critics, and thus render his book less offensive, but as we have seen, he reinforced his anti-Whig thesis at every opportunity. There was no way he was going to give up his new scene of historical thought, that insight which gave him a long awaited vocation. The only concession he made to the negative criticism the first volume elicited was to delete two passages on the "superstitious" Catholics and the "fanatical" Puritans which offended the commentator in the *Monthly Review*.[6] Rather than enfeebling his first volume, Hume responded to his critics by asking them to examine his second volume, *The History of Great Britain, Containing the Commonwealth, and the Reigns of Charles II and James II*, which he published in December, 1756. He later regretted that he did not delay the publication of the first volume until the second was ready. Had the two volumes been presented together, Hume believed that he might have avoided the reproach that he was a consistent apologist for the Stuarts, an ardent Tory, even a Jacobite.

The criticism that he was a Jacobite or passive obedience man must have piqued Hume considerably, because these comments must have been made in ignorance of, or blindness to, several of his political essays, as well as key passages in the *Treatise*, where he explicitly rejected the Jacobite and Tory positions, and adopted, in their place, a utilitarian brand of establishment oriented politics. An examination of these essays and of those parts of his philosophical works

---

[4] Hume, 1882: **3:** pp. 4-5.

[5] Hume, 1932: **1:** pp. 221-222.

[6] *The Monthly Review or Literary Journal* **12** (March, 1755): p. 207. These very same passages offended another contemporary critic of volume one, Daniel McQueen, 1756: p. 19.

where he addresses moral and political questions will reveal
what he meant when he described himself as "a Whig, but a
very sceptical one";[7] moreover, an assessment of his political
thinking at the time he undertook the second volume will
illuminate the political goals of that volume.[8]

It was Hume's essay of 1748, "Of the Protestant Succession," that prompted him to call himself a skeptical Whig. In
this essay, revising and elaborating on the definition of Whig
he had given in his essay of 1741, "Of the Parities of Great
Britain,[9] Hume gave the Whig position a new utilitarian
perspective, one that did not at all rely on traditional contract
theory. Hume encouraged acceptance of the Hanoverian
succession, because "the princes of that family . . . have, since
their accession, displayed, in all their actions, the utmost
mildness, equity, and regard to the laws and constitutions."[10]
His preference for the established Whig government was so
explicit that, owing to his past association with the St. Clair
family in Scotland, some of whom were Jacobites, he withheld the essay from publication until 1752, when the recol-
lection of the 1745 Jacobite rebellion might be more distant.[11] He later informed John Clephane that of all the
inappropriate "isms" which might be attributed to his politics, Jacobitism was the "most terrible *ism* of them all."[12]

Hume was altogether too casual in assessing his politics as

---

[7] Hume, 1942: **1:** 111. Hume here describes the position he took in his essay "Of
the Protestant Succession," which he had just written.

[8] Hume made many revisions in his political essays subsequent to the publication
of the *History*. These revisions have been traced by T. H. Green and T. H. Grose,
"The History of the Editions," Hume, 1882: pp. 73-76. Giarrizzo emphasizes these
changes because they document Hume's increasing conservatism or (according to
Giarrizzo) turn toward Toryism in the 1760's and 1770's. I am less concerned here
with Hume's pessimistic interpretation of English politics during these years than in
the status of his political thinking at the time he undertook his historical career.
   Duncan Forbes has challenged Giarrizzo's interpretation of Hume's politics, denying that Hume's politics became distinctly more conservative. On the contrary,
Forbes maintains that Hume's skeptical whiggism (which Forbes equates with scientific whiggism) amounts to an impartial and detached critique of English government (p. 135). While I do not agree with him concerning Hume's impartiality, I do
believe that Forbes does well to emphasize that all of Hume's writings—political,
philosophical, and historical—share the common goal of constructing an ideological
system that would help support the Hanoverian dynasty, but I also believe Hume's
affection for the Hanoverians is merely another manifestation of his endorsement
of "gentle" government or stable society.

[9] Hume, 1882: **3:** p. 139.

[10] *Ibid.*, p. 479.

[11] Mossner, 1954: p. 180.

[12] Hume, 1932: **1:** p. 264.

he formulated them in "Of the Protestant Succession." To declare almost flippantly that he was a skeptical Whig was to evade the significance of his adoption of a utilitarian position based on practical considerations rather than abstract theory. This type of political ideology allowed him to accept and applaud the Glorious Revolution, without ever once lending any support to the popular notion that James II had violated any original contract between the monarchy and the people. It was possible for him to extol the peaceful achievement of the parliamentarians of 1688 and still decry their innovations of the 1620's and 1640's. Hume's readers may have found this apparent inconsistency hard to understand. He had hoped that volume two of the *History* would help them, although an attentive follower of his theory on the origin and purpose of government might well have anticipated the position he was going to take on the Glorious Revolution in the *History*.

The purpose of the *Treatise,* the establishment of a philosophical basis for practical morality, had anticipated the utilitarian emphasis of his political essays. In the "Introduction" to the *Treatise,* he maintained that the science of man "will not be inferior in certainty, and will be much superior in utility to any other of human comprehension."[13] To be useful, the science of man could not be founded on any elaborate theory which could not be attested to by experience or by inferences drawn from experience. To attempt a purely theoretical system of consent or obligation, without asking whether any such theory corresponded to what we might observe of man's natural inclinations, was as futile as the search for a metaphysical foundation for knowledge or for a first cause in philosophy.

In the third volume of the *Treatise,* Hume first stated his theories concerning the origin and function of government. Like Hobbes, Hume believed that man's natural impulse is to act selfishly, without any concern for the effect of his actions on others. But by regarding social obligation from a utilitarian point of view, Hume avoided the Hobbesian necessity of resorting to a totally authoritarian form of government. Although the sense of justice is not endemic in man, it has a self-evident utilitarian appeal, since, in Hume's words, ex-

---

[13] Hume, 1882: 1: 309-310.

perience can show it to be "infinitely advantageous to the whole, and to every part."[14] Immediate gratification may remain preferable to the more obscure benefits of socially responsible behavior, but we are cable to learning to identify self-interest with the interests of society. The public good may then be felt to be coincidental with private happiness. Our capacity to develop a sympathy with public interest, Hume maintained, was made possible by the feelings of moral approbation and disapprobation which our fellows extend toward us.[15] It was this utilitarian belief, rather than any more abstract principle, which directed the formation of civil society. The peaceful state of nature, in which some form of an original contract might be consented to, was, according to Hume, "a mere fiction, not unlike that of the *golden age*, which the poets have invented."[16]

In one of Hume's earliest political essays, "Of the Origin of Government," written within a year after the publication of the last book of the *Treatise*, he restated his belief that justice is established only when men overcome their "love of the dominion of the strong," and learn from experience to prefer "the impartial administration of justice."[17] When Hume, in 1748, addressed himself to the question "Of the Original Contract," in his essay of that title, he again arrived at conclusions similar to those of the *Treatise*. There is no evidence, he wrote, "in history or experience in any age or country in the world,"[18] of a mutual agreement or voluntary association, which according to Locke, men freely assented to in a state of nature.[19] Despite his affinity for Locke's polemic against innate knowledge, Hume had to depart from Locke's theoretical assumptions on the origin of government. "The original establishment," Hume insisted, "was formed by violence, and submitted to from necessity."[20] Thus men formed civil society.

While he did not lend any credence to the typical original contract theory, Hume did believe that a type of contractual arrangement subsisted between the people and

---

[14] *Ibid.* **2:** p. 269.
[15] *Ibid.*, p. 271.
[16] *Ibid.*, p. 266.
[17] *Ibid.* **3:** p. 116.
[18] *Ibid.*, p. 447.
[19] Locke, 1960: p. 380.
[20] Hume, 1882: **3:** p. 457.

the government. Acquiescence in the established government rested on the ability of governmental institutions to
insure the public interest. The longer the government acted
effectively and felicitously, the more deference it could require of the people. Again, Hume had already provided the
logic for his political position in the *Treatise*. Here he admitted the "happy influence" of the Glorious Revolution on the
government of England. Perhaps at the time of the Prince of
Orange's accession his title or right to the throne might have
been contested, but for Hume in the 1740's, "it ought not
now appear doubtful, but must have acquired a sufficient
authority from those three princes who have succeeded him
upon the throne."[21] The Hanoverian settlement, the settlement favored by the Whigs, was therefore as morally legitimate an arrangement as there ever was.

Given Hume's respect for established government, did he
ever believe it possible to challenge or even overthrow such a
government? Addressing himself in the *Treatise* to the logic
of the Glorious Revolution of 1688, he stated the conditions
under which the people may exercise the right of resistance,
a right they retain in a limited monarchy. Attempting to
discredit any categorical notion of passive obedience Hume
wrote that "those, therefore, who wou'd seem to respect our
free government, and yet deny the right of resistance, have
renounc'd all pretentions to common sense, and do not merit
a serious answer." In the event that a king should become
"tyrannical" or "despotic," he continued, "it then not only
becomes morally lawful and suitable to the nature of political
society to dethrone him, but what is more, we are apt likewise
to think, that the remaining members of the constitution
acquire a right of excluding his next heir, and of chusing
whom they please for his successor." Hume does not say that
this had been so in the Glorious Revolution, but he hints as
much when he writes that his observations are the result of
"some philosophical reflections, which naturally arise from
that event."[22] Nor did Hume ever call either of the last Stuart
kings tyrannical or despotic; yet he did say in "Of Passive
Obedience," his last 1748 essay, that "it became necessary to
oppose them with some vehemence; and even to deprive the

---

[21] *Ibid.* **2:** pp. 327-328.
[22] *Ibid.*, p. 326.

latter formally of that authority, which he had used with such imprudence and indiscretion."[23] This essay, he thought, showed that he was no doctrinaire Tory.

In the second volume of his *History*, Hume provided the historical dimension to these philosophical reflections and to his politics, concluding that the later Stuarts deserved their fate for the very same reasons that the early Stuarts should have been spared theirs. The question of who was responsible for the upsetting of the established order depended on who unnecessarily violated traditional authority and, therefore, sacrificed a peaceful, happy, and prosperous civil state. If the type of resistance condoned by the contract theory was wrong, so were the submissive doctrines of divine right and passive obedience; the rejection of contract theory and passive obedience, expressed in the *Treatise* and in the political essays, were to be reaffirmed in the *History*. Hume's historical interpretation was anticipated both by his political theory and his ethics.[24]

A few months prior to the publication of the second volume Hume explained to Andrew Millar, who was now in full charge of overseeing the printing and sales of the *History*, that he could indeed be sympathetic in his portrayal of the first two Stuarts, and be severely critical of the last two kings of that family. His letter summarizes the theoretical consistency of his interpretation:

> The first two Princes of the House of Stuart were certainly more excusable than the two second. The Constitution was in their time very ambiguous & undetermined, & their Parliments were, in many respects, refractory & obstinate: But Charles the 2d knew, that he succeeded to a very limited Monarchy: His long Parliament was indulgent to him, & even consisted almost entirely of Royalists; yet he cou'd not be quiet, nor contented with a legal Authority. I need not mention the Oppressions in Scotland nor the absurd Conduct of K. James the 2d.[25]

Later that year he made the same point to the man who eventually succeeded Millar as his publisher, William Stra-

---

[23] *Ibid.* **3**: p. 463.
[24] Steward, 1963, is indeed correct when he writes that "the *History of England*, which by reason of its scope and artistry seems an entirely independent work . . . . is inspired by an argument drawn directly from the third book of the *Treatise*," p. 19.
[25] Hume, 1932: **1**: pp. 217-218.

han. "It was unlucky that I did not publish the two volumes together: Fools will be apt to say that I am become more whiggish in this volume: As if the Cause of Charles I and James the 2d were the same, because they were of the same Family."[26]

Hume reversed the roles of the protagonists in the second volume, where it was the king, not his opposition, who endangered the civil order by ignoring the accepted practice of the age. After a decade of Civil War and another of Interregnum, everyone in the kingdom, except the restored king, seemed to accept the idea that the English monarchy was limited. Hume did not change his principles or party allegiance in the second volume; history changed, and as a result he switched sides.

In the political essays, written before the *History*, Hume set up what has been called "an imaginary dialogue between two adversaries,"[27] with the intention of finding a moderate position for himself. Hume defined this position as skeptical Whiggism. From our perspective it seems more appropriate and helpful to interpret his politics as a rather simplistic form of utilitarianism—not the rigorous social philosophy of Jeremy Bentham, but a set of values which formed a basis for criticizing commonplace political ideologies. What is most important for us is that he needed history to explain fully his polemical critique of English politics, as well as his own moral and political philosophy. To understand that critique we should follow Hume's advice and consider his version of later Stuart history. It was, after all, in this volume that he gave "unbounded liberty in my politics."[28] He no doubt hoped that history would not only expand his study of the science of man, but make his politics and moral values clear, convincing, and popular as well.

The second volume of the *History of Great Britain* opens with a predictably derogatory account of the Interregnum. While there is a certain smugness in Hume's "I-told-you-so"

[26] *Ibid.*, p. 235. In a rather favorable review of the second volume of the *History of Great Britain*, a critic wrote that Hume was, even here, "too warm . . . to those princes of the Stuart family who have sat upon the throne of England." Despite Hume's criticism of James II, this critic thought Hume demonstrated "overstrained tenderness" in his portrait of that monarch. *Critical Review* 2 (December, 1756): pp. 385-389.

[27] Giarrizzo, 1965: p. 125.

[28] Hume, 1932: 1: p. 231.

account of how the rebellion initiated by parliamentary up-
starts ended in the erection of another form of despotism, his
opinion of the period of the Civil War was typical not only of
conservatives like Dr. Johnson but of liberal historians such
as Mrs. Macaulay and radicals like John Baxter. In commenting on Cromwell's career, Hume was content to repeat the
ancient formula that "illegal violence, with whatever object it
may pursue, must inevitably end at last in the arbitrary and
despotic government of a single person."[29] It was not
difficult for Hume to find historical evidence to support his
thesis that the steps initiated by the Commons early in the
century were radical and dangerous.

It is unfortunate that Hume's reputation as an infidel and
a skeptic kept Samuel Johnson from considering the *History*
seriously.[30] Johnson would have discovered much in that
work that was congenial to his own understanding of the
history of the seventeenth-century republican experiment.
During the period of the Puritan regime, Hume observed,
"every man had framed the model of a republic, and, however new it was, or fanatical, he was eager in recommending
it to his fellow citizens, or even imposing it by force upon
them. . . . The bonds of society were everywhere loosened."[31]
In the *Lives of the Poets,* Johnson remarked that in Cromwell's
time "any unsettled innovator who could hatch a half-formed
notion produced it to the publick": it was also a time,.he
continued, "when every man might become a preacher, and
almost every preacher could collect a congregation."[32]
Johnson even shared Hume's view of the inevitable fate of
the violence that attended both the birth and the death of the
Commonwealth. In his *Life of Milton,* he commented, "Nothing can be more just than that rebellion should end in slavery."[33]

This ignominious end of a Puritan republicanism, which
both Hume and Johnson found despicable, persuaded
Hume that "an absolute monarch" was preferable to "a re-

---

[29] Hume, 1778: **6:** p. 220.
[30] On his deathbed, Hume himself told a pestering Boswell that, despite their
other differences of opinion, "Johnson should be pleased with my *History.*" Boswell,
1970: p. 13.
[31] Hume, 1778: **6:** pp. 155-156.
[32] Johnson, 1905: **1:** p. 215.
[33] *Ibid.,* p. 116.

public in this island." Hume, again anticipating the *History*, had made this decision in his essay of 1741, "Whether the British Government inclines more to Absolute Monarchy or to a Republic." This was no abstract issue on which Hume, as an eighteenth-century political commentator, could pretend to be a disinterested observer.

> For, let us consider, what kind of republic we have reason to expect. The question is not concerning any fine imaginary republic, of which a man may form a plan in his closet. There is no doubt, but a popular government may be imagined more perfect than absolute monarchy or even than our present constitution. But what reason have we to expect that any such government will ever be established in Great Britain, upon the dissolution of our monarchy? If any single person acquire enough power to take our constitution to pieces and put it up a-new, he is really an absolute monarch; and we have already had an instance of this kind, sufficient to convince us, that such a person will never resign his power, or establish any free government.[34]

The Puritan-republican experience haunted Hume as it haunted Johnson.

It also preoccupied the pro-parliamentary history of Mrs. Macaulay. Johnson was repulsed by what he called her "absurd levelling doctrine,"[35] but neither her love of the Roman Republic nor her reformist politics permitted her to render a favorable judgment on Cromwell and his time. As much as she applauded the revolutions in France and America, she wrote that under Cromwell the nation had degenerated into "discord, faction, and their attendant evils, tumults, conspiracies, and general discontent."[36] Very late in the century, the radical John Baxter, who had been tried at Old Bailey in 1794, as a member of the London Corresponding Society, decided to write a historical tract to support his campaign for parliamentary reform. Baxter feebly attempted to render Hume's history more favorable to republican causes and Thomas Jefferson called Baxter's work "an editic expurgation"[37] of Hume, but even Baxter could not bring himself to praise the Commonwealth period.

---

[34] Hume, 1882: **3:** p. 126.
[35] Boswell, 1934-1950: **1:** p. 448.
[36] Macaulay, 1763-1768: **5:** p. 387.
[37] Jefferson, 1942: pp. 723-726. Jefferson also feared Hume's *History* because it

When William Godwin, after a long and vocal career of radical politics, decided to write a history of the civil war and Commonwealth, he recognized that the memory of seventeenth-century violence clouded the judgment of all historians of the eighteenth century, not just the conservative Hume. He was not wrong when he insisted in 1824 that "there is no part of the history of this island which has been so inadequately treated as the characters and acts of those leaders, who had for the most part the direction of the public affairs of England from 1640 to 1660."[38] As far as Godwin was concerned, the opponents of the early Stuarts had no alternative but revolution. He deliberately dissociated himself from the historians of the eighteenth century when he wrote: "The nearness or remoteness of the scene in respect of place or time, is a consideration of comparatively inferior magnitude: I wish to be wholly unaffected by the remembrance, that the events took place about a century previous to my birth, and occurred on the very soil where my book is written."[39] What was possible for Godwin writing in the nineteenth century simply was not possible for his eighteenth-century predecessors, especially for one as adamant on preserving political stability as Hume.

No matter how far apart they stood politically, most eighteenth-century British historians believed in promoting what Hume called in one of his pre-*History* essays, "a gentle government," one that avoided factionalism and extremism. Such a government, which "gives the greatest security to the sovereign as well as to the subjects, must be guaranteed to the people by the rule of law."[40] The constitutional monarchy of Britain, which had elicited praise from the French philosophes, was the type of government Hume had in mind. This is why, in his *History*, Hume, looking at the year 1660, expressed relief and joy over the Restoration of Charles II. It also explains his disappointment over the ultimate failure of the Restoration Settlement, a failure in peaceful government more the fault of the ruling family than of its opposition. For

---

"makes an English Tory, from whence it is an easy step to American Toryism," but he also thought it the finest piece of history which has ever been written by man." Jefferson's opinion of Hume is explored by Walton, 1976: pp. 389-403.

[38] Godwin, 1824: **1:** p. v.
[39] *Ibid.*, p. ix.
[40] Hume, 1882: **3:** p. 105.

Hume, as for most who lived through it, the reign of Charles II was a story of spoiled hopes.

Hume's disenchantment with the restored monarchy led him to expand his historical career in two directions. In the course of writing the history of the Restoration he used primary evidence for the first time, and he also began to communicate with another historian in order to exchange information. Hume was never very consistent in either of these pursuits as he continued to write the *History*, but his historical curiosity refutes the traditional picture of Hume writing his *History* with his feet on his sofa, utterly uninterested in documentation.[41] Although Hume did not depart from Rapin in the second volume with the same vehemence as he did in the first, he indeed introduced a new historical dimension to the history of the later Stuarts. Both Rapin and Hume condemned these kings, but it was Hume who documented the duplicity and mendacity of Charles II. Part of the satisfaction that Hume experienced in writing his second volume came from his awareness that he was expanding historical knowledge. His own need to find a career by providing new insight into the history of the Stuarts was in this instance beneficial to the historical community as a whole.

When Hume wrote his second volume, the extent of Charles's collaboration with Louis XIV and the degree of complicity of the Cabal in the secret provisions of the Treaty of Dover of 1670 were still matters of conjecture. By the 1770 edition, however, Hume was able to authenticate the conspiracy of Charles and his brother to change the national religion and subvert the Restoration government.

He obtained knowledge of Charles's connivings in the period from 1763 to 1766, in Paris where, "in spite of Atheism and Deism, of Whiggism and Toryism, of Scoticism & Philosophy,"[42] he served both as a secretary to the British Embassy and, for a time, as *chargé d'affaires*, after the ambassador, Lord Hertford, had left for the more lucrative post of lord lieutenant of Ireland in 1765. During this period, Hume gained access to the Scots College in Paris, where he

---

[41] Thompson, 1941: **2**: p. 71. Thompson charges Hume with "laziness" here on the basis of an undocumented account of his refusal to walk across the room to check a reference. The story makes for a vivid image, but it is unverifiable and misleading.

[42] Hume, 1932: **1**: p. 510.

discovered the memoirs of James II, amounting "to several volumes of small folio, all writ with that prince's own hand, and comprehending the remarkable incidents of his life, from his early youth till near the time of his death."[43] The trustworthiness of these documents has been questioned,[44] but Hume and his audience treated them as a revelation.

Hume had written in the original *History of Great Britain* that a formal alliance between Charles and Louis could explain the former's "strange measures," yet there was no direct evidence of any signed treaty or agreement. Like other historians, Hume suspected the extent of the king's intentions, but he also thought "that there was no concerted plan betwixt the two kings, and that they geverned themselves entirely by events."[45] In December, 1763, he wrote to his publisher from Paris of his discovery of King James's memoirs, and expressed the desire "to make use of them for improving & correcting many Passages of my History, in case of a new Edition."[46] In July, 1764, Hume acknowledged the cooperation of Father Gordon, principal of the Scots College, "a very obliging, communicative Man," in allowing him to consult the memoirs, and he detailed his findings:

> The Treaty was concluded in the End of 1669 or beginning of 1670 (for the Memoirs do not mark very distinctly the time) and Lord Arundel of Wardour was the Person, who secretly sign'd it, in a Journey, which he made to Paris for the Purpose. The Restoration of the Catholic Religion in England; and a Confederacy against Holland were the two chief Articles.[47]

When a new edition of the *History of England* was called for in 1770, Hume was able to replace widespread suspicion with certainty. The private provisions of the Treaty of Dover at this time became public knowledge.

The editor of Hume's correspondence has accurately noted that Hume made very few textual changes in later editions of the *History* to incorporate the information contained in the sources discovered in Paris,[48] but Hume did add the full contents of the Treaty of Dover in a footnote to

---

[43] Hume, 1778: **8:** p. 4.
[44] Lee, 1965: pp. 70-119.
[45] Hume, 1757: **2:** p. 238.
[46] Hume, 1932: **1:** p. 418.
[47] *Ibid.*, pp. 453-454.
[48] *Ibid.*, p. 455 n.

the 1770 edition; moreover, he informed another Scotsman, Sir John Dalrymple, of the treasure of historical documents in Paris, and he encouraged him to publish them. Dalrymple, whose work on feudal property in Great Britain Hume had already praised, followed Hume's lead. In 1771 he published *Memoirs of Great Britain and Ireland from the Dissolution of the Last Parliament of Charles II until the Sea Battle off La Hogue,* based on the letters and diplomatic papers in the French Foreign Office in Paris. Dalrymple's researches yielded explosive results, and Hume was among the first to learn from them. In the last edition of the *History,* relying on Dalrymple's work, Hume was able to specify the members of the Cabal who knew about the secret provisions of the Treaty of Dover.[49] The two historians profited from each other's work in detailing the sinister politics of Charles's court. This was not the last use Hume made of Dalrymple. Again, like other historians, Hume imagined that Charles was receiving a pension from Louis, but in the early editions of the *History* he had no way of documenting his suspicions. After reading Dalrymple, Hume was sure. He then wrote that Charles's pension was "one of the most dishonorable and most scandalous acts that ever proceeded from a throne."[50]

There was yet another disclosure for Hume to make on the basis of Dalrymple's *Memoirs.* Dalrymple discovered in the dispatches of Paul Barillon, the French ambassador to Charles II, that the king was not alone in his insincere patriotic protestations. Hume learned from Dalrymple that several members of the party who, in the 1670's, publicly opposed Charles's pro-French attitude, including the great Whig martyrs, Lord Russell and Algernon Sidney, executed in 1683 for their involvement in insurrectionist plots against the king, were among the secret agents and pensioners of the court at Versailles.[51] Dalrymple was more shocked by this discovery than was Hume. It taught Dalrymple, as he said in the "Preface" to the second volume of the *Memoirs,* "that there is no political party in this country which has a right to assume over another from the merit of their ancestors; it being too plain, from the following papers, that whigs and

---

[49] Hume, 1778: **8:** pp. 4-5.

[50] *Ibid.,* p. 32.

[51] Trevor-Roper, 1963: pp. 89-102, has discussed the effect of Dalrymple's discovery on the eighteenth-century Whig establishment.

tories, in their turns, have been equally the enemies of their country, when their passions and their interests misled them."[52] The conclusion to his "Preface" must have sent a shiver through the Whigs of his time: "When I found in the French dispatches Lord Russell intriguing with the court of Versailles, and Algernon Sidney taking money from it, I felt very near the same shock as if I had seen a son turn his back in the day of battle."[53] Hume already knew that neither political party had a monopoly on historical truth, and that the Whig interpretation, in particular, was marred by over-simplifications and distortions, but he took particular plea-sure in including Dalrymple's incriminating discovery in the last edition of his *History,* when he noted his amusement in observing "the general, and I may say natural, rage excited by the late discovery of this secret negotiation; chiefly on account of Algernon Sidney, whom the blind prejudices of party had exalted into a hero."[54] Hume was too skeptical to believe in heroes: his historical researches served to reinforce that native skepticism. It is no wonder that he enjoyed his new career so much.

While Hume had to substantiate his disenchantment with the behavior of Charles, no such effort was necessary for James II. Like Charles, James ascended the throne in au-spicious circumstances, and, like him, he sacrified by his own rashness the popular support he enjoyed. James managed to antagonize almost the entire population: everyone knew his actions made the Glorious Revolution necessary. Hume was in no way exceptional in endorsing the Glorious Revolution, but he did view the demise of the Stuart monarchy in a unique manner. The Glorious Revolution was not the culmi-nation of those ancient liberties which the parliamentarians had been claiming to protect against the encroachments of a despotic family. To Hume the Revolution formed "a new epoch" in the history of the constitution.

> By deciding many important questions in favor of liberty, and still more by that precedent of deposing one king, and estab-lishing a new family, it gave such an ascendant to popular principles as has put the nature of the English constitution beyond all controversy. And it may be affirmed, without any

---

[52] Dalrymple, 1773: **2:** p. vii.
[53] *Ibid.,* p. ix.
[54] Hume: **8:** p. 43 n.

danger of exaggeration, that we, in this island, have ever
enjoyed, if not the best system of government, at least the most
entire system of liberty that ever was known amongst mankind.[55]

But Hume, unlike the Whigs, refused "to decry with such
violence, as is affected by some, the whole line of Stuart; to
maintain, that their administration was one continued en-
croachment on the *incontestable* rights of the people."[56] Rapin
believed this was the case,[57] but Hume insisted that such an
interpretation was anti-historical. The revolt against James II
was entirely justified, but James's imprudent actions could
not excuse the irresponsible steps which the Commons had
taken against the first two Stuarts.

The conclusion of Hume's history of the Stuarts is as
approving of the deposition of James II as that of any Whig
historian, but his rationale for extolling that event is his own.
James II had no more violated "an original contract" (as the
parliamentarians pronounced) than Charles I had set out to
destroy established liberty. But, by flagrantly disregarding
the obvious lessons of the experience of the Civil War and
the Commonwealth, James sacrificed an established form of
government that seemed to Hume to suit public utility. Custom had made the monarchy of the 1660's a limited one; the
later Stuarts should have realized and accepted the lim-
itations inherent in the Restoration. In the philosophical and
political works which preceded the *History*, he had established in moral terms the basis for the origin and survival of
government. In the *Treatise* he wrote that all forms of government, which are founded at first only "on injustice and
violence," become "in time legal and obligatory."[58] He repeated this conviction in the *Enquiry Concerning Human Understanding*, when he concluded that "Custom, then, is the
great guide of human life."[59] When custom is respected, men
know what they can expect from one another, and from
governments. For Hume, a disregard for custom constituted
reprehensible political and immoral behavior. During the
reigns of James I and Charles I, the Commons challenged

[55] *Ibid.*, p. 320.
[56] *Ibid.* Hume's italics.
[57] Rapin, 1724-1731: **8:** p. 221.
[58] Hume, 1882: **2:** p. 328.
[59] *Ibid.* **4:** p. 39.

established practices with their bold steps. The circumstances were reversed during the reigns of the later Stuarts.

That history, politics, and moral philosophy all reinforced each other in Hume's mind—that they needed one another in order to be wholly comprehensible—is evidenced by his publication in 1758 (one year after the appearance of the second Stuart volume) of his essay, "Of the Coalition of Parties." This essay is a fusion of Hume's political and historical thinking. He here reaffirmed his rejection of the contract theory and of the doctrine of passive obedience, and added his belief that the ideological disputes between the Whigs and Tories had no firmer foundation in history than they did in moral philosophy.[60] He then offered his political credo, one he based on historical observation as much as on his political utilitarianism. "The only rule of government," he wrote,

> is use and practice . . . the sole basis of political government is not pure reason but authority and precedent. Dissolve these ties, you break all bonds of civil society, and leave every man at liberty to consult his private interest, by those expedients which his appetite, disguised under the appearance of reason, shall dictate to him.[61]

Hume thus provided a retrospective essay with the philosophical reasons for his support of the early Stuarts as well as his condemnation of the later ones.

The conclusion of this essay explained what Hume hoped would be the cumulative effect of both volumes of his history of the Stuarts on readers in contemporary Britain: "This is certain, the greater moderation we now employ in representing past events; the nearer shall we be able to produce a full coalition of the parties, and an entire acquiescence in our present establishment."[62] Hume was myopic in failing to credit the early seventeenth-century parliamentary agitators for their part in creating what he called the "new epoch" in the history of the constitution—the basis of the "present establishment"—but to have done so would have betrayed the purpose of his history and his politics. He wished to encourage the continued acceptance of a form of government he believed struck the proper balance between liberty

---

[60] *Ibid.* **3:** p. 466.
[61] *Ibid.,* p. 466.
[62] *Ibid.,* p. 469.

and authority.[63] That balance was worth preserving, even at the price of forbidding what he called, in the final version "Of the Original Contract," "violent innovations," which "no individual is entitled to make."[64] Authority and stability were more important than liberty because they guaranteed the existence of civil society.[65] Hume's account of seventeenth-century "violent innovations" was meant to make this contention as explicit as possible.

His account was also designed to emphasize his contention that established monarchy promoted economic prosperity and cultural supremacy. Republics may be laudable in the abstract, but in concrete terms, for England, at least, this type of government was detrimental to prosperity and culture. Hume believed that during the reigns of the Stuarts, England had experienced economic growth. Rapin believed the opposite to have been the case.[66] Hume's endorsement, in the *History*, of the reestablishment of monarchical government in 1660 was, in part, based on his loathing for decline of culture during the Commonwealth.[67] To him the moderation typically insured by an established monarchy was beneficial to national culture as well as to the national economy.[68]

---

[63] J. G. A. Pocock, 1971 and 1975, *passim*, suggests that the notion of a balance between extremes was a survival of Machiavellian paradigms in the eighteenth century. I have no quarrel with his insight, but have interpreted Hume's political and historical thought independently of the Machiavellian and Harringtonian traditions. Although Hume was preoccupied with the necessity for moderation in government and stability in society, he cannot be fitted into the republican tradition.

[64] Hume, 1882: **3:** p. 452.

[65] *Ibid.*, p. 117.

[66] Rapin, 1726-1731: **9:** p. 372, declared that England never flourished less than under the rule of the Stuarts. Hume, on the other hand, believed England would have prospered when James I was on the throne, if the Commons had not set out to ruin him. Hume, 1778: **6:** p. 24 and 173.

[67] In describing the "manners" of the age of the Puritan regime, Hume wrote "that the wretched fanaticism, which so much infected the parliamentary party, was no less destructive of taste and science, than of law and order. Gaiety and wit were proscribed: Human learning despised: Freedom of enquiry detested: Cant and hypocrisy alone encouraged. It was an article positively insisted on in the preliminaries to the treaty of Uxbridge, that all play-houses should be forever abolished." Perhaps Milton, who "prostituted his pen in theological controversy, in factious disputes, and in justifying the most violent measures of his party . . . had he lived in a later age," might have "attained the pinnacle of human perfection, and borne away the palm of epic poetry." *Ibid.* **8:** pp. 342-344.

[68] In the 1741 essay, "Of the Rise and Progress of the Arts and Sciences," he proclaimed that a "civilized monarchy" was most favorable to the growth of the polite arts." Hume, 1882: **3:** p. 185.

Upon publication of the history of the Stuarts, Hume believed that he had at last made his historical, political, and moral philosophy clear enough. Satisfying though that prospect must have been, it was not the case. There was more work for him to do—his career as a historian was anything but completed.

III. Tudor History and the Scottish Perspective

E VEN before the page proofs for the second volume of the *History of Great Britain* were completed, Hume was anxious about his future as a historian. His intellectual life had gained a momentum which he did not wish to stem. In June, 1756, he expressed his concern to his Jacobite friend, Lord Elibank. He wondered what his next literary project would be, "if it happen, as is probable, that Idleness becomes a Burthen to me."[1] Hume was not much charmed by idleness; indeed, he was most content when working, and now that he had found an effective vehicle, he was not about to give it up. The real question which preoccupied him was the direction of his historical studies. Would he write a history covering the period subsequent to 1688, or would he write a history of the house of Tudor?

He debated the question with himself and his friends for almost a year. He then decided to follow the example of Tacitus, who wrote the *Annals* after the *Histories,* and proceeded to write the *History of England* backwards. But the decision had little to do with his affection for Tacitus, whose writing he found so much more attractive than that of contemporary historians.[2] Although he seriously considered writing a post-Revolutionary history, he rejected the idea because he did not want to quit Edinburgh and travel to London in search of manuscripts and in pursuit of interviews with some of the men who had helped make contemporary history. He told William Mure in February, 1757, that he was too old to move,[3] but he was more candid with Adam Smith in March when he wrote of his reluctance to move to London

---

[1] Hume, 1962: p. 442.

[2] Hume was always full of praise for Tacitus, although his decision to write retrospectively was only coincidental with the example of Tacitus. More serious was his preference for the classical style. A few days after finishing his first volume he wrote to the Abbé Le Blanc "that my Narration is rapid, and that I have more propos'd as my Model the concise manner of the ancient Historians, than the prolix, tedious style of some modern Compilers." Hume, 1932: 1: p. 193. I think we can safely assume it was Rapin he had in mind as the most offensive of compilers.

[3] *Ibid.,* p. 243.

in order to "find materials sufficient to ascertain the Truth"
for a history of his own time.[4] Mure and Smith, as fellow
Scotsmen, must have understood Hume's apprehension—
London at mid-century was not hospitable to visitors from
"North Briton," especially to those with literary ambitions.
James Boswell was to discover this in the next decade, and he
was considerably more thick-skinned than Hume. That it was
not really a matter of being too old to move is demonstrated
by Hume's enjoyable and profitable sojourn to Paris after the
History of England had made him a luminary in the Republic
of Letters. Considering how openly and bitterly Hume had
criticized the factious Whig ministries, his fear of applying to
Whig statesmen for help is quite comprehensible.[5]

Hume's wish not to return to London, where he had spent
the most miserable year of his life as tutor to the marquess of
Annandale, was an important initial factor in deciding to
continue the history retrospectively, but, by May, he had
found an even more compelling reason to write a history of
Tudor England. He informed Millar that he had begun the
reign of Henry VII and gave him two reasons for his choice.
The first was his insistence that at this time "modern history
commences. America was discovered: Commerce extended:
The Arts cultivated: Printing invented: Religion reform'd:
And all the Governments of Europe almost chang'd." The
distinction between modern and medieval history, that is,
between accessible, instructive history and obscure, myth-
ridden history, was becoming standard historical periodiza-
tion at this point in the age of Enlightenment; Voltaire had
recently promulgated it in the opening pages of *Le Siècle de
Louis XIV*, and Hume was an ardent admirer of that popular
work.[6] The second reason was even more significant for
Hume; it implied what was to become one of the central
purposes of the Tudor volumes. "I wish," he continued to his
publisher, "therefore I had begun here at the accession of

---

[4] *Ibid.*, p. 246.

[5] Even after the *History* had been completed Hume never overcame his fear of
approaching the Whig aristocrats. One reason he gave for not writing a sequel to his
work was: "I cannot hope to finish the Work in my Closet, but must apply to the
Great for Papers and Intelligence; a thing I mortally abhor." Hume, 1954: p. 71.

[6] Hume, 1932: 1: p. 226. Hume here makes the pertinent observation that he was
not Voltaire's pupil, even if he was an admirer of the Frenchman, who was more
interested in cultural developments—his main energy was focused on refuting the
Whigs' understanding of the constitution.

Henry VII at first. I should have obviated many Objections, that were made to the other Volumes."[7] Hume did not specify which objections he had in mind, but in a few months' time, when he was working assiduously on the first of the Tudor volumes, a main theme of his interpretation of Tudor history emerged. What he would have to say about the history of the Tudors would reinforce what he had already written of the Stuarts. He soon came upon the realization that there was no better way to prop up an anti-Whig history of the seventeenth century than to ground it in a history of the preceding century that was designed to highlight the inconsistency of the Whig interpretation.

Although Hume was at work on the next segment of the *History* in May, he was still, in August, searching for a specific focus. Even after finishing the reign of Henry VII, he was somewhat uncertain as to how he could take another swing at the Whigs. He confided to Minto that he was making "a tolerable smooth, well told tale of the History of England during that period; but I own I have not yet been able to throw much new Light into it."[8] One month later that light burst forth. Dr. John Clephane, Hume's physician friend of ten years, was the first to learn about it. Just as he had written to Dr. Cheyne concerning his conversion to a new scene of thought in renouncing the study of law for philosophy as an adolescent, and in a manner resembling that in which he had written to Adam Smith describing his discovery of a new career as a historian, Hume imparted his latest discovery with delight and excitement. He told Clephane he wished he had begun the *History* with the reign of Henry VII, "for by that means, I should have been able, without making any digression, by the plain course of narration, to have shown how absolute was the authority which the English kings possessed, and that the Stuarts did little or nothing more than continue matters in the former tract, which people were determined no longer to admit."[9] Hume promised Clephane that as soon as he had finished with his latest production he would visit him in London. And once Hume had found his "new light" he was able to work happily, without interruption for over a year. By the autumn of 1758, a new work of

[7] *Ibid.*, p. 249.
[8] *Ibid.*, p. 264.
[9] *Ibid.*

history was born, and, in writing it, Hume once again showed the vitality of a productive scholar.

There was nothing particularly arresting in the observation that the Tudors had been more absolute than their Stuart successors. But Hume expanded on the obvious; he made it the main development in English constitutional history for the entire Tudor period, and more than that, he was delighted to be able to expend his energy in making Tudor despotism a convincing historical foundation for his controversial interpretation of Stuart history. Everyone, including the Whigs, had praise for the great Queen Elizabeth. Hume wished to vindicate his controversial Stuart volumes and show the Whigs how unhistorical it was to adulate one arbitrary princess while condemning the Stuart princes who emulated her maxims. In January, 1759, when the Tudor *History* was about to be published, he wrote to William Robertson, "You will see what light and force this History of the Tudors bestows on that of the Stuarts. Had I been prudent I should have begun with it. I care not to boast, but I will venture to say, that I have now effectually stopped the mouths of all those villainous Whigs who railed at me."[10] It is apparent that by this time Hume had become obsessed with leveling the Whigs. He became continually more open in his hatred, without much actual justification. There had not been *that* much adverse reaction to either of his Stuart volumes, but apparently Hume needed an adversary in order to be productive. The Whigs fulfilled that function.

This association with Robertson signaled another motive for Hume to write the Tudor volumes: the desire to influence the course of Scottish history. Robertson's *History of Scotland* was published just six weeks before Hume's Tudor history;[11] and in some respects, the proximity of publication dates reflected a common purpose, a purpose they shared with other Edinburgh literati in the 1750's. Hume had made it clear in his second Stuart volume, and in his essay, "Of the Coalition of Parties," that he favored an acceptance of the established Hanoverian Succession in England. Readers of his Tudor volumes discovered that his message for Scotland

---

[10] *Ibid.*, p. 294.
[11] Robertson's *History of Scotland* was published in January, 1759, and Hume's *History of England under the House of Tudor* in March. Unlike their Stuart predecessors, both volumes of Tudor history appear together, the second volume being entirely devoted to the reign of Elizabeth.

was less passive. The forces of reaction were very much alive when Hume was writing, and he joined with Robertson in an effort to discredit them. The Jacobite rebellion of 1745 had been remarkably successful, despite the efforts of moderates like Robertson, who left his study for the only time in his life to help defend Edinburgh against the army of the Stuart Pretender with its highland chiefs. In the decade after the rebellion, Hume, Robertson, and a whole society consisting of liberals within the General Assembly of the Kirk, such as the Reverend Hugh Blair, and of lapsed Jacobites like Lord Kames, banded together in an effort to modernize Scots culture, language, and religion.

In the Tudor volumes, Hume expended a good deal of energy in de-romanticizing some of the legends associated with the sixteenth century, both in England and in Scotland. His efforts here should be understood as part of the program of the Edinburgh Enlightenment, which was the cultural milieu out of which the *History* grew. The men who led that movement believed that Scotland's future lay with a vigorous acceptance of the union with England, a healthy purging of the Scots dialect, and of suppression of everything that was clannish, parochial, and backward. They had a very sober view of Scots history. They realized that prior to the union, Scotland was isolated and poor. The hegemony of the Kirk had precluded the possibility of education for Scotsmen in papist Paris; those in search of a liberal education had to enter the universities of Holland, if they could afford it. At the beginning of the eighteenth century, Englishmen referred to Scotland as "terra incognita,"[12] and they were not exaggerating. The roads from London to Edinburgh were barely passable, the journey took at least two weeks, and, upon arrival, a visitor from the south would encounter a filthy city where violence and drunkenness were obvious. If a foreigner were curious enough to explore country life, he would find pervasive poverty and frugality—the result of ignorance or prejudice against every innovation in agricultural technique. A trip to the Highlands would allow a glimpse of the feudal society of the great Highland chiefs with their pretentions and credulity. This was the Scotland the Enlightenment wished to bury.

Gradually, after the Revolution of 1688, which regener-

---

[12] Graham, 1928: p. 2.

ated contact with the Dutch, and after the Union of Parliaments in 1707, necessitated in part by the Darien disaster (the abortive Scottish attempt at empire, the country's economic ruin), the situation began to improve. By mid-century, the increased contact with England and Holland had tempered the severity of Knox's theology; the Jacobite rebellion had been suppressed at great cost and the Highland chiefs had been deprived of some of their ancient privileges. The Turnpike Road Act of 1751 meant that the post could be delivered within a week's time from London, and that the journey to the north would no longer be such a dreadful trek.

Mid-century was seen as the turning point; some progress had been made, but much more remained. When Hume returned to Scotland, was elected Keeper, and began his *History*, he joined the clubs that campaigned for improvement in the areas in which the country had been particularly deficient before the Union. The "Preface" to the *Edinburgh Review* of 1755 presented a précis of the pattern of Scottish history as seen by the literati:

> From this state of langour and retardation at the Union of Crowns in every species of improvement, Scotland soon passed thro' a series of more dreadful evils. . . . Amidst all the gloom of these times, there were still some men who kept alive the remains of science, and preserved the flame of genius from being altogether extinguished. At the Revolution, liberty was reestablished, and property rendered secure; the uncertainty and rigor of the law were corrected and softened: but the violence of parties was scarce abated, nor had industry yet taken place. What the Revolution had begun, the Union rendered more compleat. The memory of our ancient state is not so much obliterated, but that by comparing the past with the present, we may clearly see the superior advantages we now enjoy, and readily discern from what source they flow. The communication of trade has awakened industry; the equal administration of laws produced good manners; and the watchful care of the government, seconded by the public spirit of some individuals, has excited, promoted and encouraged, a disposition to every species of improvement in the minds of a people naturally active and intelligent. If countries have their ages with respect to improvement, North Britain may be considered as in a state of early youth, guided and supported by the mature strength of her kindred country.

The authors of this progressive piece maintained that the two greatest obstacles to improvement of culture were the lack of a "standard of language" and a deficiency in "the art of printing." To redress these faults, this review of literature proposed to "give a full account of all books published in Scotland within half a year; and to take some notice of such books published elsewhere, as are most read in this country, or seem to have any title to draw the public attention."[13]

The supporters of the *Edinburgh Review* were able to publish only two numbers of their little journal, which had such ambitious and comprehensive aims; however, the importance of the production is evident even in the "Preface." The publication reflected the goals of the literati of Edinburgh, who sought the improvement of Scottish society. Improvement meant encouraging contact with the rest of Europe, especially in literature and commerce, but it was not to be confined to these general cosmopolitan causes; it was to touch on the most mundane problems of agriculture, medicine, or even baking. The most distinguished of these clubs was the St. Giles or Select Society formed by the painter Alan Ramsay. They met for the first time on Wednesday evening, May 22, 1754, and they chose for their meeting place the Advocates' Library; their host was David Hume. Hume had already been secretary to the Philosophical Society, which was now to be replaced by a gathering of even more practical-minded intellectuals that included his friends. They agreed to meet every week on Wednesday nights, and so they did until 1763, the year after Hume had presented the complete *History of England.*[14]

The extant minute books of the Select Society contain the rules and procedures by which the Society conducted its meetings and also list the questions to be debated. Though the actual content of the debates is omitted, the questions themselves tell us how widespread the interests of these literati were.[15]

Adam Smith chaired the meeting of June 19, 1754, and he announced the subjects for debate for the following week: "Whether a general naturalization of foreign Protestants

---

[13] *Edinburgh Review* 1 (July, 1755): pp. i-iii.

[14] "Rules and Orders of the Select Society," MS. 23.1.0: p. 1.

[15] Whatever is known of the meetings of these societies is discussed by D. D. McElroy, 1969.

would be advantageous to Britain? Whether Bounties on the exportation of Corn be advantageous to Trade and Manufactures as well as to Agriculture?" That same evening it was "ordered that David Hume, Esq., be, and he consenting, thereby is appointed Treasurer to the Society, and that he receive and give out the Society's money as he shall see cause, and that he give in his Account once every year."[16] On December 4, 1754, Hume presided. The minutes for this meeting are the neatest in the book, and the question discussed was "Whether ought we prefer ancient or modern manners with regard to the conditions and treatment of Women?" While this question still arouses heated differences of opinion, the questions debated in the following months reflected very clearly the intellectual and political interests of the men of the Scottish Enlightenment. On December 11, 1754, they asked "Whether the differences of National Characters be chiefly owing to the nature of different Climates; or to moral and political causes?" It was Hume, who, after reading *De l'esprit des lois,* with great excitement, congratulated its author and arranged to have parts of it published in Edinburgh in 1750. Two months after the discussion of Montesquieu's sociology, the Society debated an issue set out in what was almost the verbatim title of one of Hume's first political essays. Hume listened as his friends considered "Whether the Liberty of the Press ought not be restrained?"[17]

The Select Society served as a model for the Edinburgh Society for Encouragement of Arts, Sciences, Manufactures, and Agriculture, which met for the first time in March, 1757. According to the *Scots Magazine* for that year, this group of literati did more than talk. They offered cash prizes for such achievements as "the best dissertation on the nature and operation of manures"—the author in this instance was to receive a silver medal as well as money. They offered five guineas "to the person who shall cure and preserve in a dry form, the greatest quantity of yeast, so as still to be fit for the purposes of brewing and baking, not under ten pounds weight, to be produced before the first February next."[18] Like its prototype, the Edinburgh Society did not neglect the

---

[16] "Minutes and Procedures of the Select Society," MS. 23.1.1: pp. 15-16.
[17] *Ibid.,* pp. 33-46.
[18] *Scots Magazine* (March, 1757): pp. 160-161.

discussion of literary topics; it rewarded authors of the best essay on taste and insisted on the use of good English. Both societies published articles containing regulations for promoting the reading and speaking of the English language in Scotland. Similar topics occupied the Belles Lettres Society, which added to its membership roster the names of Adam Ferguson and William Robertson.[19] This society, formed in January, 1759, the very month Robertson's *History of Scotland* was published, pondered the new sociology (which would eventually emerge as a new sociological history in Robertson's *America*), as well as the superiority of the moderns over the ancients, and the advantages of luxury; that is, of comfort and material progress.

The program for improvement was immense in scope, but Hume and his associates were devoted to the cause of Great Britain: Scotland's dark age had to be revealed as having been miserable. The advantages of the Union, of free trade, and of a modern language had to be impressed upon all those who would listen. It was a tribute to the Scottish Enlightenment and to Robertson's liberality and cosmopolitan spirit that he concluded the first national history of his country with a condemnation of chauvinism and a celebration of the Union. "Thus, during the whole seventeenth century," he wrote,

> the English were gradually refining their language and their taste: in Scotland, the former was much debased, and the latter almost entirely lost. . . . Even after science had once dawned upon them, the Scots seemed to be sinking back into ignorance and obscurity. . . . At length, the union having incorporated the two nations, and rendered them one people, the distinctions which had subsisted for many ages gradually wear away; peculiarities disappear; the same manners prevail in both parts of the island; the authors are read and admired; the same entertainments are frequented by the elegant and polite; and the same standard of taste, and or purity in language, is established. The Scots . . . were at once put in possession of privileges more valuable than those which their ancestors had formerly enjoyed; and every obstruction that had retarded their pursuit, or prevented their acquisition of literary fame, was totally removed.[20]

---

[19] "Proceedings of the Belles Lettres Society," MS. 23.3.4: p. 1.
[20] Robertson, 1851: **2**: pp. 323-324.

It was indicative of the spirit of the age that this same historian, when he became principal of the University of Edinburgh, gave himself over to the task of modernizing the outdated curriculum and of renovating the squalid buildings.

Most of Hume's campaign for the modernization of Scotland is implied in the second of the Tudor volumes, where he set out to denigrate the reputation of Mary, Queen of Scots. Both Robertson and Hume believed that, if ever Scotland were to enter completely the modern age, the romantic attachment to the heroine of the Highlanders and Jacobites would have to be cast away. In the first volume of Tudor history, which covers events from the accession of Henry VII to that of Elizabeth, Hume demonstrated similar anti-romantic points of view in regard to English history.

Hume's first opportunity of attacking the Jacobite fascination for a legendary past arose while he was writing the history of Henry VII. Just as the first Tudor monarch was settling himself on the English throne, his dynasty was challenged by the Flemish-born Perkin Warbeck, who claimed to be the Duke of York, younger son of Edward IV. Warbeck spun an incredible tale of how he had been spared the murderous wrath of Richard III, while his brother had been slain by agents of that villainous king. Hume was, of course, incredulous, and there was nothing exceptional about his lengthy attack on Warbeck in the first edition of the Tudor history—he was merely following the example of Tudor historians from More to Bacon who had all denounced Richard III for his perfidy and Warbeck for his imposture. But Hume's motivation was special. In the early 1750's Thomas Carte, a Scotsman and an ardent Jacobite, who had participated in the uprising of 1715 and who had refused to declare allegiance to George I, published four folio volumes of *A General History of England*. It was a carefully researched, but in some ways an absurd, undertaking. Carte wanted to demonstrate that the English kings exercised authority which might be traced back to the Druid priests. Carte sought to disparage those writers who supported the establishment of an institution with as defective a pedigree as the Tudor monarchy. Those historians, Carte maintained, represented "Richard III as a monster," and wrote only "to blanch the conduct of Henry VII, and exalt his character by unmerited elogiums."[21] Hume, unlike Carte, had little interest in dynastic pretensions; his admiration of Henry was based on the fact that the first Tudor had brought peace to his adopted kingdom.

It was not surprising that Carte, the active supporter of an authentic pretender in the eighteenth century, gave credence to the claims of a preposterous pretender of the fifteenth. When Hume sided with More and Bacon in the polemic against Warbeck, he was making an effort to discredit the remaining supporters of the reactionary Jacobite party in England, who swore by the Stuarts and at the Hanoverians. The contrast between Carte and Hume suggests that a divergence of political attitudes or historical perspectives bespeaks contrary temperaments and philosophies. Carte seems to have preferred a continuation of the Wars of the Roses and a rebellion on behalf of the Stuarts, in the attempt to place a time-honored dynasty on the throne. For all the weakness of their dynastic titles, Hume welcomed the establishment of both the Tudors and the Hanoverians; the name of the ruling family could be Welsh or German: what mattered to Hume was the practical result of the settlements.[22]

While Hume was revising the 1770 edition of the *History*, he came upon a document which he was able to use in support of his contention that there was little to romanticize in the annals of English history. It was Adam Smith who provided Hume with *The Regulations and Establishment of the Household of Henry Algernon Percy, the Fifth Earl of Northumberland*, edited by the antiquarian, Thomas Percy. Hume was now armed with evidence that any kind of Whig ancestor worship of an Arcadian past was unrealistic, if one considered how most of the population subsisted. The servants of the Northumberland household, for example, Hume learned,

> eat salted meat almost through the whole year, and with few or no vegetables, had a very bad and unhealthy diet: So that there cannot be any thing more erroneous than the magnificent ideas formed of the Roast Beef of Old England. We must

[21] Carte, 1747-1755: **2**: p. iv.
[22] Hume expanded the attack on Warbeck in his 1770 edition of the *History*. He reinforced his original argument as a response to Horace Walpole's, 1768. Hume, 1778: **3**: pp. 456-457.

entertain as mean an idea of its cleanliness: Only seventy ells of
linen at eight-pence an ell are annually allowed for this great
family: No sheets were used: This linen was made into eight
table-cloths for my lord's table; and one table-cloth for the
knights.[23]

Thomas Percy was embarrassed at Hume's exposure of the
parsimonious management of the earl's family. He did not
think that his antiquarian labors would be used in quite this
way. After obtaining a pre-sale copy of the 1773 edition of
the *History*, he wrote to Hume, asking him either to delete the
references to "our Household Book," or at least to add a few
kind words about his ancestor, who had been, for his time, a
magnanimous man. "I do not by any means desire that you
should deviate one jot from truth or justice," he pleaded with
Hume, "but I simply apprehend that, consistent with both,
you may place the whole subject in a more favourable light,
and, upon a revisal, will find that they rather demand it."[24]
Hume pretended to be sympathetic to the appeal. The day
he received Percy's letter he wrote to Strahan expressing
concern over Percy's misunderstanding of the reason for
which he was citing the *Household Book*. Hume did not intend
a "Satyre on that particular Nobleman. . . . I only meant to
paint the manners of the Age."[25] Hume responded to Percy
also on the day he received Percy's "complaining, but obliging" letter, and he made precisely the same point.

> It never was my Idea, that the Earl of Northumberland was
> more *niggardly* or more *stately* than other Men of his rank in
> England: On the contrary, the chief Curiosity of this House-
> hold Book is, that, by giving us a general Insight into the
> Manners of the Age, it throws a great Light upon that Period.
> . . . My Notion is, that the uncultivated Nations are not only
> inferior to civiliz'd in Government, Civil, military, and
> ecclesiastical; but also in Morals; and that their whole manner
> of Life is disagreable and uneligible to the last Degree. I hope
> it will give no offence (and whether it do or not, I must say it) if
> I declare my Opinion, that the English, till near the beginning
> of the last century, are very much to be regarded as an
> uncultivated Nation; and that even *when good Queen Elizabeth
> sat on the Throne*, there was very little good Roast Beef in it, and

---

[23] *Ibid.*, p. 461.
[24] *Calendar of Hume MSS:* **6:** p. 81.
[25] Hume, 1932: **2:** p. 267.

no liberty at all. . . . Why still exalt Old England for a Model of
Government and Laws; Praises which it by no means deserves?
And why still complain of the present times, which in every
respect, so far surpass all the past.[26]

Hume's satire is undeniable, but his goal went beyond making Percy uncomfortable: the past had to be understood in a
disenchanted manner in order for the present to be appreciated, and modernization encouraged.

Delighted as he was to demonstrate that times were hard in
Tudor England, Hume was even more adamant in under-
scoring the relatively pliant nature of Tudor parliaments.
Both Henry VII and Henry VIII fascinated him because
they appeared to encounter so little opposition from the
Commons. During the reign of Henry VII, Hume believed
that monarchical government became "more absolute" than
it had ever been.[27] Hume's interest in the Henrician Reformation stemmed chiefly from what he believed to be Henry
VIII's single-handed achievement in defying papal authority. He detected acquiescence, not collaboration, on the part
of Parliament both in the king's divorces and his break with
Rome. A submissive group of men, they acted as the king
requested: they sent to the Tower whomever he designated,
they passed bills of attainder upon command, and they
agreed, without a flinch, to his divorces. According to Hume,
this king "sported with law and common sense," and Parliament followed him in "all his caprices."[28] Hume obviously
overstated his case: Henry received credit in his *History* for
accomplishments we know were the product of a coopera-
tive, but not submissive, Parliament, to say nothing of the
work of Thomas Cromwell. What interests us, however, is
not Hume's oversimplification, but rather the use he made of
the notion of Tudor despotism: he saw it as bolstering his
case against the Whigs and putting his Stuart volumes on
firmer ground. Rapin too saw Henry as having "an absolute
grip over his subjects,"[29] but Rapin also believed that James I
had been more absolute than any of his predecessors. Hume
thought he had hit on a fundamental inconsistency in the
Whig argument, and he was right.

[26] Hume, 1954: pp. 197-199.
[27] Hume, 1778: **3:** p. 395.
[28] *Ibid.*, p. 459.
[29] Rapin, 1726-1731: **7:** p. 525.

The writing of the history of the reign of Elizabeth afforded Hume the opportunity of venting his animosity against the Whigs in a new direction. While he steered clear of writing Scottish history (that was Robertson's assignment and they did not want their works to overlap), he did have to address those aspects of that history that affected England. One which he apparently delighted in recounting was the story of the Reformation in Scotland. Hume's pleasure at being able to unmask the hypocrisies and oppressive character of the Scottish Reformation and its leader lends yet another dimension to his position as an anti-Whig historian. While his diatribes against the Queen of Scots established his credentials as an anti-Jacobite historian in Scotland, he hoped that his account of the Scottish Reformation would show that he was no Whig, for Mary's irrational behavior did not make her Calvinist enemies any more attractive to him. Upon publication of the Tudor volumes, he asked Robertson to inform Walter Goodall, a confirmed Jacobite and alcoholic, who spent much of his time in the Advocates' Library dozing and doing research to counteract the effect of Hume's *History*, "that if he can but give me up Queen Mary, I hope to satisfy him in every thing else; and he will have the pleasure of seeing John Knox and all the Reformers made very ridiculous."[30] The same sentiment inspired him to quip ironically to Adam Smith a month later:

> In recompense for so many mortifying things, which nothing but truth could have extorted from me, and which I could easily have multiplied to a greater number, I doubt not but you are so good a Christian as to return good for evil; and to flatter my vanity by telling me, that all the godly in Scotland abuse me for my account of John Knox and the Reformation.[31]

The origin of Hume's loathing for the Whiggamore Kirk is not hard to find. The brand of Calvinism which Knox imported into Scotland emphasized the darker aspects of an already grim theology. During Hume's childhood the impoverished state of Scotland tended to make the austerity of Calvinism even more pervasive and depressing. One histo-

---

[30] Hume, 1932: 1: pp. 299-300. In an earlier letter to Adam Smith (July 28, 1759), Hume maintained that his Tudor history should give equal offense to Whigs and Jacobites alike. *Ibid.*, p. 314.

[31] *Ibid.*, p. 320.

rian has given us a vivid account of Scottish Calvinism in the eighteenth century.

> The Sunday acquired in Scotland a sanctity which far exceeded that of the Sabbath of the Jews in their most Pharisaical days—equalling in austerity the Puritanism of New England, and surpassing the Puritanism of England, from which much of the Scottish superstitious veneration for the day was unhappily derived. . . . Civil and ecclesiastical authorities went hand in hand in disciplinary measures. Acts of Parliament, resolutions of Town Councils, and decisions of Sherifs supported the Church. Municipal laws in Edinburgh forbade barbers to shave the heads of gentlemen, or carry their periwigs to them, on Sabbath, under penalty; also the loitering in the streets under fine of half a rix dollar *toties quoties;* and even the idle gazing out of windows on the Lord's Day entailed a fine.[32]

It is likely that Hume attended the three-hour sermons at the Chirnside Parish, where the Ninewells household was registered. Chirnside itself had been a center of Covenanting; and the minister, George Hume, young David's uncle, was an ardent Calvinist, whose father died a martyr for the faith. The prescribed sermon, preached every Sunday, included a reaffirmation of the Fall, the present helpless and sinful condition of man's state, the slight hope of redemption, a future life for the elect, and eternal damnation for the many. When Hume left Ninewells for Edinburgh, where he attended the University from the impressionable age of twelve to fourteen, he found a religious atmosphere as oppressive as that at Chirnside.

The most popular preacher in Edinburgh was Thomas Boston, and he was renowned for his Cromwellian type of Puritanism.[33] On his deathbed, Hume told a disappointed Boswell that, although he had read the Calvinist *Whole Duty of Man,* he had abandoned any religious belief after he had begun reading Locke and Clarke. But it is close to impossible to make such a clean break. Hume never quite forgave nor forgot, in his adult life, the gloomy Calvinist environment he experienced as a child. No wonder then that, as a historian, he found so much pleasure in making the Reformers look ridiculous.

---

[32] Graham, 1928: pp. 314-317.
[33] Kemp Smith, 1948: pp. 1-8.

Hume's antipathy for the Scottish reformers helps to ex-
plain why he was sympathetic to the plight of Mary, Queen of
Scots, when she first appeared in his work. He expressed a
good deal of compassion for the young queen at the time she
was forced to leave France and rule over the Scotland of
Knox and the Covenanters. Until Mary took up with
Darnley, Rizzio, and Bothwell, Hume saw her as a victim of
Knox's "cant, hypocrisy, and fanaticism."[34]

The lurid details of Mary's involvement with a series of
worthless lovers need not be recounted. Hume believed that
she was guilty of murdering Darnley and set out to prove it
with untypical zeal. The case against Mary rested on the
authenticity of the Casket Letters, documents which, Mary's
enemies maintained, proved that she was Bothwell's mistress
before Darnley's murder, and that together they planned the
assassination of her husband. That these were Mary's letters,
and not forgeries, has never been accepted as the simple
truth by all historians, but Hume believed in them because he
wanted to destroy the reputation of the patroness saint of the
Jacobite party, whom he called a whore and a murderess. To
demonstrate the authenticity of the Casket Letters, Hume
used, for the first time, manuscripts that were in the Advocates' Library.[35] Hume was willing to do this type of research
if the polemical effect warranted it, and it did here.

Hume's diatribe against Mary caused quite a stir, which
pleased him enormously. In 1760, William Tytler, a member
of the Select Society, writer to the Signet, and friend of
Walter Goodall, the Jacobite, produced a tedious and legalistic defense of Mary in response to Hume. Tytler insisted
that Mary's enemies conspired to kill Darnley and then heap

[34] Hume, 1778: 5: pp. 23-24.
[35] The manuscript collection at the National Library of Scotland includes the
entire collection of the Advocate's Library, which it replaced. Hume's precise reference is now listed as "Adv. MSS. 35.1.1."; originally it was "A. 3.28. p. 314." These
manuscripts are copies of the originals which were part of the Cotton Library. They
concern Scottish affairs from the period of Mary's arrival in Scotland to the time of
her execution. The specific letter which Hume cites does indeed mention the fact
that Norfolk thought that the Casket Letters were genuine. Hume did not travel to
England to see the originals; there is no evidence that he ever went that far to
corroborate his assertions, but he was proud of his use of manuscripts and primary
sources—when they came his way or when he could send for them. He concluded
this exhaustive (and exhausting) footnote, emphasizing, "It is proper to observe that
there is not one circumstance of the foregoing narrative, contained in the history,
that is taken from Knox, Buchanan, or even Thuanus, or indeed any suspected
authority." *Ibid.*, pp. 497-501.

to the blame on their faultless queen.[36] Tytler was not alone in coming to the defense of Mary at the time of Hume's assault. In 1965 the National Library of Scotland obtained a refutation of Hume's indictment of Mary far more carefully presented than Tytler's. The authorship of this manuscript has not as yet been determined,[37] but whoever wrote this response to Hume revealed, by the vehemence of his work, that Hume had irreparably damaged the pride of the Scottish Jacobites and of all Scots who refused to bury the past. The author replies, line by line, to Hume's condemnation of Mary for her part in her husband's murder. The references correspond to the 1759 edition of the Tudor History, the very time when Hume was promoting anti-nationalist causes in Scotland and the literati in general were promoting modernization.

In *My Own Life*, Hume noted rather gleefully that his version of the reign of Elizabeth "was particularly obnoxious," but added that he had by 1759, "grown callous against the impressions of public folly."[38] Again the autobiography makes Hume appear more detached than he really was. His reaction to Tytler showed him to be anyting but callous. Hume said Tytler's reply to his *History* "from beginning to end, is composed of such scandalous artifices; that no one ought to believe him." He enlarged upon his criticism of Tytler in the final edition of the *History* adding that Scots Jacobites, who maintain the innocence of Queen Mary, "must be considered as men beyond the reach of argument and reason, and must be left to their prejudices."[39] Hume was gentler on his friends who were Jacobites, but nonetheless insistent that they renounce their folly. To Lord Elibank he wrote:

> It is an old Proverb, *Love me, love my Dog:* But certainly it admits of many exceptions; I am sure at least, that I have a great Respect for your Lordship; yet have none at all for this Dog of yours. On the contrary, I declare him to be a very mangey Cur:

---

[36] Tytler, 1760: p. 262.

[37] The title page of the manuscript reads "Sir J. Steuart's Observations on Hume's History Relative to Q. M. Stuart." MS. 321.68. It was thought that Sir James Steuart, the Scots political economist, was the author, but it is now certain that the manuscript is not in his handwriting. Dr. T. I. Rae, assistant keeper in the Department of Manuscripts, thoughtfully brought this manuscript to my attention.

[38] Hume, 1882: **3:** p. 6.

[39] Hume, 1778: **5:** p. 504.

Entreat your Lordship to rid your hands of him as soon as
possible: And think a sound beating or even a rope too good
for him.[40]

The response to Hume's volume on Elizabeth, whether from
friends or enemies, shows how deeply *engagé* the work was.

So was Robertson's. Just as the two historians suffered
together adverse criticism of outraged partisans of the
Queen of Scots, such as Tytler, they worked together to
establish her guilt. The year before Robertson's *History* appeared, Hume congratulated Andrew Millar on contracting
with Robertson to publish a "Work of uncommon Merit." "I
know," Hume wrote, "that he was employ'd himself with
great Diligence & Care in collecting the Facts: His style is
lively & entertaining: And he judges with Temper and Candor." Hume was also gratified that Robertson, benefiting
from his own fiasco with Hamilton and Balfour, went directly
to Millar.[41]

Although they agreed on the authenticity of the Casket
Letters and all that they implied, Hume was unable to persuade Robertson that James remained loyal to his mother,
and that she had played an active role in the Babington
conspiracy. Hume was convinced that, by the time of her trial
for her role in the Babington conspiracy, Mary had become
totally irrational, and he looked for proof that James remained as loyal and pious a son as could be expected of
such a treacherous mother. Despite her attempt to have him
kidnaped (and Hume was adamant that she willingly consented to such a scheme),[42] Hume believed that James's behavior at the trial was perfectly correct; moreover, he was
annoyed that Robertson simply did not do his homework
properly. "You told me," Hume wrote to Robertson before
the publication of the *History of Scotland*, "that all historians
had been mistaken with regard to James's behaviour on his
mother's trial and execution, that he was not really the pious

---

[40] Hume, 1932: 1: p. 321.

[41] *Ibid.*, p. 273.

[42] Hume insisted that the evidence for the conspiracy was contained in a letter
from Mary to her confidant, Charles Paget. The historian claims to have seen the
letter, which had been part of the collection of Patrick Forbes, who had published a
series of letters in 1740. It appears that the letters passed into the hands of Lord
Royston, an antiquarian, to whom both Robertson and Hume acknowledged a great
debt. Hume further insisted that the collection of Burghley State Papers, edited by
William Murdin, corroborated this theory. Hume, 1778: 5: p. 508.

son he pretended to be." Robertson made this assertion on
the testimony of the French ambassador, Courcelles, and
told Hume that John Campbell, a historian living in London,
had shown him Courcelles's manuscript. Hume, forever
skeptical, went to see Campbell.

> I accordingly spoke of the matter to Dr. Campbell, who
> confirmed what you said, with many additions and amplifica-
> tions. I desired to have the manuscript, which he sent me. But
> great was my surprise, when I found the contrary in every
> page, many praises bestowed on the King's piety by both Cour-
> celles and the French Court; his real grief and resentment
> painted in the strongest colours. . . . What most displeased me
> in their affair was, that as I thought myself obliged to follow
> the ordinary tenor of the printed historian, while you appealed
> to the manuscript, it would be necessary for me to appeal to
> the same manuscripts, to give extracts of them, and to oppose
> your conclusions. . . . I immediately concluded that you had
> not read the manuscripts but had taken it on Dr. Campbell's
> word.[43]

Hume had, on a previous occasion, consulted the copies of
the Cotton Library manuscripts at the Advocates' Library, to
prove that James had never been a party to his mother's
many schemes against the English queen.[44]

Perhaps it was Hume's affection and sympathy for James I,
who was almost a tragic hero in the first Stuart volume, that
inspired him to correct his friend's mistakes; however, he
found it even more important to convince Robertson that
Mary was no naïve dupe of Babington's evil scheming. While
it could not be doubted that Mary was somehow involved in
the Babington conspiracy, her defenders maintained that
Walsingham forged the actual letter which proved she consented to the assassination plan. Hume first argued that
there was every logical reason to assume Mary's guilt, given
her character and her past actions.

> She believed Elizabeth to be an usurper, and a heretic: She
> regarded her as a personal and a violent enemy: She knew that
> schemes for assassinating heretics were very familiar in that

---

[43] Hume, 1932: 1: pp. 288-289.

[44] Hume, 1778: 5: p. 254. The manuscript Hume cites is a copy of a letter to
Walsingham from the Scottish court asserting that James "never agreed to an
association with his mother, and that his mother had never gone further than some
loose proposals." MS. 35.1.1: p. 401.

age, and generally approved of by the court of Rome and the
zealous: Her own liberty and sovereignty were connected with
the success of this enterprise.

Then Hume moved from logic to formal proof; his source
was the *State Papers* edited by Thomas Murdin. What put
"her guilt beyond all controversy," Hume insisted, was the
letter Mary wrote to Thomas Morgan on July 27, 1586,
which Murdin published. In this letter, which Hume quoted,
Mary speaks of the treasonous correspondence with
Babington and of her willingness to help in the plot in any
way she could. For Hume this document confirmed the case
against Mary.[45]

Hume tried to get Robertson and the publisher, Millar, to
stop the production of the *History of Scotland,* in order to
make room for the new evidence.

> What I wrote to you with regard to Mary's concurrence in the
> conspiracy against Queen Elizabeth, was from the printed his-
> tories of papers; and nothing ever appeared to me more evi-
> dent. . . . But now I am sorry to tell you, that by Murden's [*sic*]
> State Papers, which are printed, the matter is put beyond all
> question I got these papers during the holidays, by Dr. Birch's
> means; and as soon as I had read them, I ran to Mr. Millar and
> desired him very earnestly to stop the publication of your
> History till I should write to you and give you an opportunity
> of correcting a mistake of so great a moment; but he absolutely
> refused compliance. . . . Your best apology at present is, that
> you could not possibly see the grounds of Mary's guilt, and
> every equitable person will excuse you.[46]

Hume was equitable because Robertson and he were, in his
own words, "heroes" together;[47] if Robertson would not
cooperate, Hume still would not criticize him openly on this
issue. On the contrary, he recommended Robertson's *History,*[48] and in the end simply regretted that they both had
"drawn Mary's character with too great softenings."[49] For his

---

[45] Hume, 1778: 5: pp. 510-513.

[46] Hume, 1932: 1: pp. 290-292.

[47] *Ibid.,* p. 300.

[48] *Ibid.,* p. 344.

[49] *Ibid.,* p. 299. In this letter Hume asks Robertson to consider specifically the
evidence regarding Mary's scheme to have her son kidnaped and placed in the
hands of the Catholic powers. "You will see in *Murden* [*sic*] proofs of the utmost
rancour against her innocent, good-natured, dutiful son. She certainly disinherited
him. What do you think of a conspiracy for kidnapping him. . . ."

part, Robertson, rather meekly, held that circumstances prejudiced the English court against Mary,[50] and he declined to alter his story to include Hume's discoveries.

From the historiographical perspective, this flurry of correspondence impels us to revise the notion that it was Robertson rather than Hume who was consistently interested in manuscript sources and factual accuracy. It is true that Hume generally expended energies in these directions when he could promote his polemics as a result—this was the case in his use of James II's memoirs, which he unearthed in Paris, and a similar situation existed here. No matter how sporadic his interest in primary sources, it should be recalled that Hume could demonstrate "the true instinct of the researcher"[51] upon occasion, and that history as a science was the better off for his efforts.

Hume's interpretation of the opposition to Elizabeth in the Commons was designed to reinforce his anti-Whig argument that liberty in England was no older than the seventeenth century. In the 1580's and '90's the classical Puritan movement was led by Peter Wentworth. He dared speak out on issues such as freedom of speech in the Commons, and even went so far as to press the queen to declare openly a successor. Elizabeth responded to Wentworth by having him sent to the Tower. Later champions of Wentworth have emphasized his courage; Hume pointed to his ultimate defeat. He wrote that Elizabeth conducted herself more like "a Turkish divan"[52] than an English queen in her encounters with Wentworth and other members of the opposition. He further insisted that her ultimate victory over the Commons in all controversies constituted "proof at what a low ebb liberty was at that time in England."[53]

Whigs like Rapin presented a confusing picture of the reign of Elizabeth; they admitted she was arbitrary (how could they deny it); and yet joined in the general praise continually bestowed on that greatest of English monarchs. Rapin, while having duly recorded Elizabeth's triumph over the parliamentarians, wrote that the English then "were the

---

[50] Robertson, 1851: **2:** p. 273.

[51] J. B. Black, 1926: p. 119, maintains that Robertson rather than Hume possessed this instinct, but he was wrong.

[52] Hume, 1778: **5:** p. 441.

[53] *Ibid.*, p. 532.

happiest people under the sun. They saw no designs upon their liberties, nor any infringement of their privileges encouraged."[54] In the "Appendix" to the history of the Tudors, Hume, having proved how arbitrary and well loved Elizabeth was, seized upon the illogical nature of the Whig interpretation. "The party amongst us who have distinguished themselves by their adherence to liberty and a popular government, have long indulged their prejudices against the succeeding race of princes, by bestowing unbound panegyrics on the virtue and wisom of Elizabeth."[55] Rapin praised the arbitrary Elizabeth, and, at the same time, reproached the first two Stuarts for subverting the constitution, and for the unprecedented extremes of their arbitrary rule. Hume demonstrated that there were many in the Elizabethan Commons who thought they enjoyed precious little liberty, and that the first two Stuarts feebly and unsuccessfully emulated the autocracy of the last Tudor.

When his career as a historian was just beginning, Hume wrote that "the misfortune of a book, says Boileau, is not the being ill spoke of, but the not being spoke of at all."[56] While the reaction to the Stuart volumes did not wholly allay his fear of being ignored, the reaction to the Tudor volumes brought him immediate fame. Much of the notoriety achieved by his history of the Tudors came from his detractors, such as Richard Hurd, who was clever enough to observe in his *Morals and Political Dialogues*, published the same year as Hume's Tudor volumes, that Hume "judged it necessary to the charm, to reverse the order of things, and to evoke this frightful spectre [of absolute power] by writing (as witches used to say their prayers) *backwards*."[57] Hurd's slur was not easy to ignore; Hume was amused by it himself. He remarked to Adam Smith that Hurd's abuse was proof that "The Whigs . . . are anew in a Rage against me."[58] Hume planned no response to Hurd—his history would have to speak for itself. By the end of 1759 Hume had gained the recognition he confessed to Minto the year before he wanted

[54] Rapin, 1727-1731: **9**: pp. 214-215.

[55] Hume, 1778: **5**: p. 451.

[56] Hume, 1932: **1**: p. 214.

[57] Quoted in *ibid.*, p. 313. There seems to be some doubt as to the authorship of the remark. See Stockton, 1971: p. 279. There is no doubt, however, that the remark was made, and that is most important.

[58] Hume, 1932: **1**: p. 214.

so much. At that time he told Minto that authors write for public applause, and that a reward in the afterlife had no significance for him.[59]

It is ironic but perhaps true that Tudor history brought Hume too much acclaim. When, in 1765, Hume was removed from his post at the British Embassy in Paris, he speculated that one of the reasons for his dismissal was that he had offended Grenville by his insistence that "Elizabeth's Maxims of Government were full as arbitrary as those of the Stuarts . . . a Proposition . . . contrary to the Principles of sound Whiggery."[60] It was unrealistic for Hume to expect to remain there after the Duke of Richmond, that great oak of Whiggery, had replaced Lord Hertford, who had arranged for Hume's initial appointment. But Hume's statement does show us how large a role the *History* was to play in his image of himself.

Hume had promised Dr. Clephane that once he had completed the volumes on the Tudors he "would write no more. I shall read and correct, and chat and be idle, the rest of my Life."[61] But this was not to be. When Hume discovered that the Whigs could be faulted in their interpretation of the Middle Ages, he decided to continue writing history backwards.

---

[59] *Ibid.* 1: p. 278.
[60] *Ibid.*, p. 502.
[61] *Ibid.*, p. 264.

IV. The Middle Ages and the Ancient Constitution

I N SOME respects it may seem curious, even ironic, that Hume ever consented to write a history of medieval England. We know that he believed that any history worth admiring as well as recounting after the fall of Rome began in the early Renaissance, with that fortunate set of circumstances which permitted what he termed "a revival in learning and commerce." He shared the philosophes' open contempt for the myth-ridden Middle Ages—to them a barbaric period of powerful priests and credulous superstitious peoples. Moreover, he would have to encounter the perennial problem of which all medievalists despair, the obscurity and paucity of sources, at least for the period prior to the twelfth century; yet he undertook his medieval volumes without the desire or temperament required to study and master the philological skills necessary to use whatever primary material might be uncovered.

He was induced to take up the task by his publishers who, for the first time, offered him an advance. But his decision was more influenced by his need to be active intellectually than it was by money—his Tudor volumes sold well and sales of the Stuart volumes improved as a result. Still Hume had to go on, for as he had explained to John Clephane, in announcing his new career as a historian, "there is no happiness without occupation,"[1] and, as it turned out, no occupation had brought him more happiness than that of historian. The option of continuing the *History* into his own time was out of the question: he never overcame his disdain of applying to Whig statesmen for information.[2] Thus the Middle Ages became his next assignment.

---

[1] Hume, 1932: **1**: p. 170.

[2] After the publication of the complete *History of England,* both Hume and his publisher Strahan were plagued by proposals from hacks to continue the work. Strahan pleaded with Hume to do it himself: "It is the only thing wanting to fill up the measure of your Glory as the Great Historian and Philosopher of the Eighteenth Century." *Ibid.* **2**: p. 243n. Hume was not persuaded, but he was relieved that the

At first he approached the medieval volumes with apparent aloofness, not unlike the detached attitude he expressed when he first began to write Tudor history. In the summer of 1759 he informed Adam Smith:

> I signed yesterday an Agreement with Mr. Millar; where I mention that I proposed to write the History of England from the Beginning till the Accession of Henry the VII: & he engages to give me 1400 pounds for the Copy. This is the first previous Agreement ever I made with a Bookseller. I shall execute this Work at Leizure, without fatiguing myself by such ardent Application as I hitherto employed. It is chiefly as a Resource against Idleness, that I shall undertake this Work: For as to Money, I have enough: And to Reputation, what I have wrote already be sufficient, if it be good: if not, it is not likely I shall now write better. I found it impracticable (at least fancy'd so) to write the History since the Revolution.[3]

But just as it had been with the Tudor volumes, Hume was not able to sustain his indifference. By the spring of the following year, he took a different tone with regard to writing about the Middle Ages. He wrote to Millar, "I am very busy & am making Progress; but find, that this Part of English History is a Work of infinite Labour & Study; which however I do not grudge: For I have nothing better nor more agreeable to employ me."[4] He then proceeded to ask for an exhaustive supply of books, which were not in the Advocate's Library, to be sent to him "with the first Ship." His catalog consists of some of the most important works of medieval scholarship, including Thomas Hearne's new edition of *Doomsday Book*. He also requested Sir Robert Cotton's collation of the *Tower Records* and whole sets of Anglo-Saxon and Anglo-Norman *Chronicles*, which were not printed until

---

assignment went to Smollett rather than to Macpherson, whom he had always regarded as a complete fraud. At one point he asked Adam Smith: "Have you seen Macpherson's Homer? It is hard to tell whether the Attempt or the Execution be worse. I hear he is employed by the Booksellers to continue my History: But in my Opinion, of all men of Parts, he has the most anti-historical Head in the Universe." *Ibid.* **2:** p. 280. Earlier in his career, Hume had effectively challenged the authenticity of Macpherson's whole Ossian hoax in an unpublished essay, "Of the Authenticity of Ossian's Poems," Hume, 1882: **4:** pp. 415-424. Hume withheld his excellent critique of Ossian out of affection for his friend, the Rev. Hugh Blair, who seemed to believe it all.

[3] *Ibid.* **1:** p. 314.
[4] *Ibid.*, p. 321.

the Rolls Series appeared in mid-nineteenth century. Quite
unexpectedly Hume was becoming a medievalist.

By November or December, 1760, he was deeply engaged
in medieval history as he had been in both Stuart and Tudor
history. With the mild euphoria that seemed to overcome
him whenever he was working hard, he wrote to Strahan: "I
am wholly engrossed in finishing my History; and have been
so above a twelvemonth. If I keep my Health, which is very
good and equal to any Fatigue, I shall be able to visit you in
eight or nine Months."[5] What was it that transformed a
casual undertaking consented to as an anodyne against idleness into a work that wholly engrossed its author? It was the
discovery—made almost by chance as many of Hume's historical insights were gained—that the intellectual foundation
of the Whig interpretation, the ancient constitution, could be
effectively challenged in a narrative history of the Middle
Ages. Once he believed that he could again criticize the
Whigs' shibboleths, he had no trouble meeting the deadline
he set for himself. In November, 1761, the two volumes of
medieval history, from the invasion of Julius Caesar to 1485,
were published, and in 1763 the *History* was published as a
whole for the first time.

The Whigs in their *grand siècle* praised the Revolution of
1688 precisely because it was not revolutionary; it was, historians, politicians, and sycophants echoed, a reassertion of
ancient liberties which had existed from time out of mind,
and which the lately deposed Stuart family had tried to
subvert. The ancient constitution, the Whigs insisted, was the
envy of Continental Europe, where despotism had flourished
in its absence. In 1724, John Oldmixon, an orthodox Whig
historian, undertook his *Critical History of England,* in order to
preserve "our present happy Constitution," and to inform
his readers of "the Antiquity and Strength of our Constitution," and show them "how it has been preserv'd from the
First of Time to our own, against the Assaults of Power and
Priestcraft." Oldmixon was sure his audience would be gratified to congratulate themselves at having been shielded
from "Continental Slavery" by a priceless, indigenous institution.[6] It was just this type of whiggish self-approbation that

---

[5] *Ibid.*, p. 335.
[6] Oldmixon, 1724: pp. 1-3.

Hume had scorned and ridiculed in the volumes of the *History* already published. In the early volumes he would attack the historical arguments on which seventeenth-century lawyer-parliamentarians and their eighteenth-century heirs based their claims concerning the antiquity of the Commons and the continuity of the common law—that timeless and venerable object of adulation, the ancient constitution.

The relation between the common law interpretation of the seventeenth century and the Whig interpretation of the eighteenth has been precisely stated by J.G.A. Pocock. "The common law mind," personified by Coke, Pocock writes,

> may be termed the common-law interpretation of English history, the predecessor and to a large extent the parent of the more famous Whig interpretation. It arose from latent assumptions governing historical thinking, assumptions which had been planted deep in the English mind by centuries of practice of a particular form of law; but it possessed also a political aspect, the need to make a case for the "ancient constitution" against the king.[7]

Pocock attributes the insularity of Coke's interpretation to the absence of a basis of comparison with Roman law and feudal custom, which formed part of the Continental legal tradition. One of the consequences of the common-law interpretation was an absolute refusal on the part of seventeenth-century lawyer-parliamentarians to acknowledge the Norman Conquest and to give a reasonable date for the origin of the Commons. For evident reasons, opponents of royal prerogative maintained that the laws of England had remained unchanged through generations of Saxons, Danes, and Normans. As Pocock has observed, during the Stuart period "the more that came to be known about remote ages, the more vigorously it was insisted that the law was before Abraham."[8] Before Pocock, Herbert Butterfield lamented that "in England we made peace with our Middle Ages by misconstructing them," meaning that the Whigs after the Glorious Revolution celebrated "that freedom had been perfect in Anglo-Saxon times. Liberty did not in fact have to be

---

[7] Pocock, 1967: p. 46.
[8] *Ibid.*, p. 37.

created or hatched or evolved or nursed into existence. It only needed to be restored."[9]

The controversy over the Conquest and the immemorial origins of the Commons reached its peak in the 1680's when Charles II was criticized in the Exclusion Parliaments; however, historians such as William Atwood and William Petyt, the king's adversaries, left a permanent mark on English historical thinking. Behind Burke's passion for prescriptive rights and the nineteenth-century Whigs' love of the uninterrupted, progressive growth of English institutions culminating in a great, liberal state, lies that convenient fiction of an ancient constitution perpetually renewed. For Burke's generation, it has been well noted that "the interpretation of history which that doctrine necessitated—involving the assertion that Magna Carta confirmed the laws of Edward the Confessor, which were themselves no more than a codification of law already ancient—had, as Burke remarks, been constantly put forward by lawyers from Coke to Blackstone."[10] It is true that Blackstone in his *Commentaries* hung on to the myth of the ancient constitution well after Hume had discredited it, maintaining that the rights of Englishmen were as old as creation and that Magna Carta was little more than a reaffirmation of these rights. Citing Coke as his authority, Blackstone repeated the bromide that "the absolute rights of every Englishman . . . are coequal with our form of government." He had nothing but praise for the "ancient Constitution" of "our Saxon forefathers."[11] What Blackstone had elevated with learning a popular essayist could boast of with vulgar enthusiasm just a few years later: "If ever God did concern Himself about forming a government for mankind to live happily under, it was that which was established in England by our Saxon forefathers."[12] Almost a century earlier Petyt had boasted: "This so famous and so excellently constituted Government is the best polity upon Earth."[13] In some quarters, whiggish chauvinism had continued unabated. Not only did lawyers and essayists hold

---

[9] Butterfield, 1944: pp. 7 and 34.
[10] Pocock, 1971: p. 208.
[11] Blackstone, 1783: 1: p. 127, and 4: p. 420. This is the ninth edition "with the last corrections of the author." The *Commentaries* were first published in 1765-1769.
[12] *Historical Essay in the English Constitution* (1771), quoted in Briggs, 1959: p. 9.
[13] Petyt, 1680: p. 78.

on to the notion of the ancient constitution in the eighteenth century—both before and after Hume discredited it—so did historians. In the 1790's, the radical historian, John Baxter, criticized Thomas Paine for failing to realize that English liberty did not have to be defended by any doctrine of inherent or natural right, but rather by its ancient roots in the Saxon period.[14]

As a foreigner, Rapin was less enamored of the ancient constitution than native propagandists like Oldmixon. But for all his hesitations and bows to impartiality, Rapin did believe that "whatever changes have occurred in other European nations, the English constitution has remained the same,"[15] and this insistence on the fundamental continuity of English institutions and customs, from Saxon times to the Glorious Revolution, was indeed the hallmark of Whiggery. Even William Guthrie, whose history was published only a few years before Hume's and who, like Rapin, wished to stay away from the more egregious whiggish assumptions, believed in the ancient constitution.[16]

The Whigs' insistence on the continuance of an ancient constitution did not pass into the eighteenth century without criticism, prior to Hume's assault. As I mentioned earlier, in chapter one, the pamphlet war against Walpole in the 1730's, led by Bolingbroke, forced ministerialist writers to assume a rather anti-Whiggish position. The *Craftsmen* for the year 1730 vehemently insisted on the ancient rights of Englishmen. The government press had no choice but to take the opposite stance. In 1734 Lord Hervey, refuting Bolingbroke, insisted, as Hume would twenty years later, that there was no liberty in England before the Glorious Revolution.[17] But not much attention was paid to an in-house critique. When Hume raised the standard against the ancient constitution, there was, in the memorable words of Duncan

---

[14] Baxter, 1796: 1: p. ix.

[15] Rapin, 1727-1731: 1: p. i.

[16] Guthrie's belief in the ancient constitution is nowhere more evident than in his Dissertation III, "Concerning the Norman Engraftments upon the English Laws and Government," which is appended to the third and final volume of his *History of England*, published in 1751, just a year before Hume started to write his *History*. The people, wrote Guthrie, always "carried in their eye" the principles of the Saxon constitution right down to the reign of James I (p. 1387). Hume makes no reference to Guthrie, nor does Guthrie's *History* seem to have attracted much attention from other readers.

[17] Hervey, 1734: p. 40.

Forbes, "an outcry from the Whigs as though the ark of the covenant had been defiled."[18] The sacred cows of the Whigs were very much alive when Hume tried to kill them, and, despite his campaign, they still were not beaten to death.

Hume first reflected on the nature of the ancient constitution when he wrote the appendix, "The Anglo-Saxon Government and Manners," in the first of the medieval volumes. Understanding the relation between the prerogatives of the various Saxon kings and the rights of the people was difficult enough—the period encompassed seven kingdoms over a period of six centuries. Hume's impatience with the "monkish chroniclers" who were his chief sources did not make the job any easier for him. All he felt he could be certain of was the violent temper of the times making any established principles of government impossible. The tenor of any particular Saxon government was determined by the fortuitous succession of kings and not, as typically held by the Whigs, by immemorial rights endemic to the ancient tribes. If the king were strong like Alfred the Great, he could dominate the Witenagemot; if the king were weak, like Edward the Confessor, he would be dominated by the council. In no case could the constitution be considered as a fixed body of laws guaranteeing "a regular plan of liberty" or anything else.

As far as Hume was concerned, the Saxon constitution was as crude and as simple as that, yet he knew the issue of the composition of the Witenagemot could not be settled simply. Party histories, he insisted, had obfuscated the matter with spurious certainty. The debate over the composition of the council was as much a matter of a party feud as it was a historical controversy. And Hume was glad to enter both. "The matter," he wrote, "would probably be of difficult discussion, even were it examined impartially; but as our modern parties have chosen to divide on this point, the question had been disputed with greater obstinacy, and the arguments on both sides have become, on that account, the more captious and deceitful." The "monarchical faction," he continued, believed that, in addition to noblemen, only judges or lawyers were part of the council. "The popular faction assert them to be representatives of the boroughs, or what we now

---

[18] Forbes, 1976: p. 249. Forbes has an economical and well-focused summary of the historiographical debate of the 1730's, pp. 241-249.

call the commons."[19] With ample condemnation made of
party prejudice, Hume proceeded to side with the opponents
of the "popular faction." The boroughs "were so small and so
poor, and the inhabitants lived in such dependence on the
great men, that it seems nowise probable they would be
admitted as part of the national councils."[20] The source for
this piece of polemical history is listed as "Brady's Treatise of
English Boroughs." The information regarding the other
groups in the Witenagemot is noted as having been drawn
from the entry "parliamentum" in Spelman's *Glossarium Ar-
chaiologium.*

As Hume's medieval history unfolds, he comes more and
more to rely on the works of Sir Henry Spelman and Sir
Robert Brady in asserting the impact of the Norman Conquest, the introduction of feudal law in Anglo-Norman England, and the origin of the Commons in the thirteenth
century. He did not have to ask Millar to send him the works
of these seventeenth-century historians—they were very well
known, and already in the Advocates' Library, as indeed they
should have been.

Spelman's most important contribution to English historiography was his discovery, in his *Archaeologus* of 1626,
that feudal burdens were first integrated into English law by
William I. He maintained, in that work, that feudal obligations and customs, such as the hereditary feudum, the rights
of wardship, and the tradition of homage simply did not exist
in a typically feudal sense before the Conquest. Spelman was
able to establish these observations by examining the meaning of the various terms which the Anglo-Saxons used to
designate their obligations to their kings, in opposition to
what the subjects of Anglo-Norman Britain meant. He stud-
ied the terms of office and obligation in their contemporary
context, comparing the variety of meanings in Anglo-Saxon,
Vandal, Gothic, German, and Norman French; thus he ex-
posed the anachronistic contention by which seventeenth-
century lawyers insisted that Anglo-Saxon precedents were

---

[19] Hume, 1778: 1: p. 201. Atwood, Petyt, and James Tyrell had all insisted that
Commons were part of the Witenagemot.

[20] *Ibid.,* p. 202. Rapin, 1727-1731: 2: p. 173, debated the issue whether or not the
Witenagemot was comprised of the Commons and was ultimately ambiguous on the
issue. In the "Preface" to volume one, he did maintain that the Saxon council was an
"assembly of all the nation." Oldmixon, 1724: p. 26, had no doubt that the Commons were part of the council "from the time of Edward the Confessor."

valid for their own political struggle with the crown.[21] Hume
demonstrated how Spelman's labors could be put to excellent
use: the members of the Witenagemot simply could not be
compared to members of Parliament. The meaning of the
terms he learned from Spelman was far too disparate. Seldom has a glossary been as well employed as Spelman's was
by Hume.

Unlike Spelman, Sir Robert Brady believed that feudalism
had no precedents at all in the Saxon period,[22] and unlike
Spelman, his researches yielded openly polemical results,
which made them all the more attractive to Hume, when he
popularized them sixty years later. Brady's career was as
political as it was historical. During the Civil War, he had
been declared a traitor; his property was confiscated, and he
eventually joined the king in exile. His loyalty was well rewarded: in 1660, by virtue of a special patent from the king,
he became physician ordinary at court and professor of medicine at Cambridge, as well as master of Caius College at the
same university. With Fabbian Phillips and William Dugdale,
Brady wished to expose the historical errors Atwood and
Petyt had used to support the Commons in their conflict with
the king. For example, in the *Of Cities and Burghs* (1690)
Brady intended to justify the Stuart attack on municipal
liberties by demonstrating that the Commons were of far
more recent origin than the Whig historians maintained. In
his own words, the aim of his work was to show that

> the Original Constitution of Burghs . . . was not Eternal or at
> least Coaeval with Creation. . . . But whoever shall peruse this
> Treatise, shall find the Dates of their Originals, and Gradual
> Augmentations, and must confess that they have nothing of
> the Greatness and Authority they boast of, but from the
> Bounty of our Ancient Kings, and their Successors, notwith-
> standing any other Confirmations, or acquired Right, they may
> allege, and acknowledge that Prescription, and pretended
> Immemorial Customs or Usages avail not, when there are
> Charters or other Records which show, that in this case, they
> are mere Conjectures, Words of Course, and the popular
> assertions of such Men, as either knew not how, or would, or

---

[21] Pocock, 1967: pp. 93-99.

[22] Pocock makes the important point that although Spelman saw feudalism as a
normal importation in the *Archaeologus*, he did believe feudal law was a confirmation
of the laws of Edward the Confessor; thus Spelman "pours new wine into old
bottles" in 1627 in his *Codex Legum Veterum. Ibid.*, p. 107.

for their more gainful Imployments could, not look into those great Monuments of Antiquity, and discoverers of Truth.[23]

This work made Spelman's discovery of feudalism a permanent part of seventeenth-century historiography designed to support the claims of the monarchy against the parliamentarian-lawyers and historians.

The Treatise on Boroughs was not the only work in which Brady attacked the large body of pseudo-historical literature, typified by *Argumentum Anti-Normanicum,* which appeared in 1682 when Charles II was under attack in Parliament. William Atwood, a Whig barrister, was probably the author of this diatribe against the authority of the king, whose main point is obvious enough: "William I never made an Absolute Conquest of the Nation; he did not abolish all the English laws; or take away the estates of the English, there were English men in the Common Council of the whole kingdom.' "[24] The bulk of Brady's *Complete History of England* had two purposes: to prove that the contemporary Commons had no history either in Saxon or in Norman times, and to establish the fact that the Norman Conquest reduced England to a feudal barony. "Sir Edward Coke, and all late Writers when they chop up upon these times," he wrote, cannot tell "where or when their Fundamental Rights" originate.[25] Brady's critical method was similar to Spelman's: he examined the records of the past in the effort to understand the meaning of the words and institutions to the men who wrote in those times. His polemical intention notwithstanding, Brady's accomplishments were a necessary corrective to the simple-minded assertions of Atwood and his contemporary, William Petyt. For his part Petyt had declared—with unflinching certainty and no proof—that "in the British, Saxon, and Norman Governments, the Commons (as we now phrase them) had Votes, and a share in the making and enacting of Laws for the Government of the Kingdom . . . before and after the supposed Conquest by King William the First."[26]

Brady, of course, fell from favor after the flight of James II. In March, 1689, Brady, member of Parliament and keeper of the Tower records, was ordered to surrender the

[23] Brady, 1690: pp. i-ii.
[24] Atwood, 1682: p. cxv.
[25] Brady, 1685: 1: p. iii.
[26] Petyt, 1680: pp. 73-74.

key to this repository of historical documents to his arch-
enemy, Petyt, whose work he had spent so much energy
refuting.[27] The reaction against Brady began with James
Tyrell, who in the 1690's undertook a *History of England* with
the express purpose of discrediting him.[28] Tyrell, a close
friend of John Locke,[29] never finished the *History*, but he did
not have to—that seems to have been the implicit expectation
of most Whig historians until Rapin. Hume was the first in
the eighteenth century to write a constitutional history of
medieval England that was systematically and seriously devoted to restoring the Brady tradition.

Hume introduced the subject of the Norman Conquest
itself in his concluding remarks on the government of
Anglo-Saxon England. Even though he had insisted that the
distinguishing feature of that government was its unsettled
character, he nevertheless detected a comparatively strong
aristocratic influence in anything approaching affairs of
state, especially after the abolition of the Heptarchy, when
the king lived so far from the great landholders that he could
exert but little influence on them.[30] It is logical to assume that
Hume made this observation in part to support his contention that the effect of William's Conquest was to reverse this
trend. He also underscored his contention that feudalism as
it was known on the Continent was altogether absent in
England before the Conquest. Hume saw no evidence of
feudal law—no homage, wardship, reliefs, or any of the
other ceremonies and institutions usually present in feudal
governments. The Saxons had no use for these institutions
because they did not need the type of military establishment
on which the feudal hierarchy was predicated. Since they had
destroyed the ancient Britons, there were no insurrections to
suppress, but Hume was quick to point out that William's
situation was different; the Norman prince needed and used

---

[27] Pocock, 1951: p. 202.

[28] Tyrell, 1698-1704: **2**: p. cv.

[29] Curiously enough the work of Locke does not fit into this controversy because
he never took on Brady directly. As Peter Laslett had remarked, "Locke made no
appeal to his history or tradition." "Introduction," to Locke, 1965, p. 2. Perhaps it
was Locke's lack of historical discussion that distinguished his political works from
the corpus of Whig history that Hume openly attacked. Hume does challenge
Locke's political theory, as I discussed in Chapter II.

[30] Hume, 1778: **1**: p. 204.

the feudal law he brought with him when he landed at Hastings.[31]

In stressing the impact of William's Conquest, Hume used every argument and bit of evidence he could find. He found his most impressive material in Brady. The aspect of the Conquest Hume chose to emphasize above others was William's suppression of the nobility, and he could find the support he needed in Brady. Whether they resisted or acquiesced in William's rule, the ancient and wealthy families of the Saxon era were reduced to poverty. In a footnote to his description of William's usurpation of lands belonging to the Saxon nobility, Hume wrote:

> There is a paper or record of the family of Sharneborn, which pretends, that that family, which was Saxon, was restored upon proving their innocence, as well as other Saxon families which were in the same situation. Though this paper was able to impose on such great antiquaries as Spelman and Dugdale, it is proved by Dr. Brady (see answer to Petyt) to have been a forgery; and it is allowed such by Tyrrel, though a pertinacious defender of his party notions.[32]

While disputing Petyt's insistence on the ancient origin of the Commons as well as his denial of the Conquest, Brady had uncovered many inaccurately cited or improperly used documents, such as the one referred to by Hume.[33] This forgery afforded Hume the irresistible opportunity of reminding the great Whig aristocrats that their family histories might not be as old or as unblemished by poverty or humiliation as they may have wished to believe.

Considering William's achievements, Hume asked how "some writers" might have been "desirous of refusing to this prince the title of Conqueror, in the sense which that term commonly bears?" Only the prejudices of party history, he answered rhetorically, could blind historians to William's violent and sudden alteration of power and property. "These facts are so apparent from the whole term of the English history, that none could elude them, were they not heated by

---

[31] *Ibid.,* pp. 224-229.

[32] *Ibid.,* p. 478.

[33] Brady, 1681: p. 30. The whole book is devoted to exposing forgeries or fraudulently used evidence, as the author explains in his "Advertisement to the Impartial and Judicious Reader."

the controversies of faction; while one party was *absurdly* afraid of those *absurd* consequences, which they saw the other party inclined to draw from this event."[34] If we consider the tone of the anti-Conquest literature, most saliently exemplified by the statement in *Argumentum Anti-Normanicum,* "thus we can see the Mighty Conqueror is himself conquered, and solemnly renouncing all Arbitrary Will and Power, submits his will to be regulated and governed by Justice, and the ancient Rights of Englishmen,"[35] it is hard to resist agreeing with Hume's assessment of the historiographical controversy. Brady was far more sober in discussing the reality of the Conquest than either the historians like Atwood and Petyt whom he reproached, or the ones, like Tyrell, who sought to criticize him. It may have been that Hume sided with Brady as much out of an abhorrence for the Whigs' hyperbolic style as out of his desire to rekindle the polemics of the seventeenth century, and place himself in the Brady tradition.

The period between the Conquest and Magna Carta was of little interest to Hume; yet he found one point he could make to bolster his anti-Whig argument. As part of his program to demonstrate that few legitimate precedents for restricting the prerogatives of the monarchy existed in this period, he stressed that Henry I's Coronation Charter was a meaningless gesture, intended to placate the barons, but in fact granting them nothing, because the king "never once thought during the reign, of observing a single article."[36] The Coronation Charter was sometimes invoked as a precedent for Magna Carta, thus allowing it to become part of the ancient constitution. To Hume it was no such thing. Even if Henry had been sincere in his intentions, his Charter could not be used as a precedent for the establishment of new laws or liberties at a later date, say the seventeenth century. This was too rude a period for laws, written or not, to be respected. At this point in English history, "laws had very little influence: Power and violence governed everything."[37] The laws of the Middle Ages, such as they were, could not be analogous to the laws of modern England, because the times themselves

---

[34] Hume, 1778: 1: p. 283.
[35] Atwood, 1682: p. xxx.
[36] Hume, 1778: 1: p. 316.
[37] *Ibid.*, p. 216n.

were too dissimilar. Here was another occasion for Hume to expose an anachronism and a false analogy: the stuff of which the Whig interpretation was made.

When the barons exacted Magna Carta from King John at Runnymede in 1215, they claimed to be reasserting their traditional rights which a despotic king had violated. "The barons," the historian wrote, "demanded of the king, that in consequence of his oath before the primate, as well as in defense to their just rights, he grant them a renewal of Henry's charter, and a confirmation of the Laws of St. Edward."[38] A confirmation indeed. According to Hume, the baronial demands of the thirteenth century were no more a confirmation of existing law than were the innovations sought by lawyers of the seventeenth century, which they, in turn, had insisted were their rights from time immemorial. Hume maintained that Henry I's Coronation Charter was not a valid precedent for Magna Carta because, like the coronation charters before it, the promises made at coronation were chiefly ceremonial; nor were there any Saxon liberties to be restored. He had made sure of that in his history of the Heptarchy, and even if there were traces of aristocratic privilege in Saxon times, they were certainly eliminated, or at least attenuated, by the devastating Conquest and the introduction of feudal law. The barons at Runnymede resented the king's unpopular taxes, yet he asked for little more than his father or brother before him. Because he was a defeated and vulnerable monarch, he was susceptible to what Hume thought was the false charge that he had violated rights; he therefore had to sign the document.

If Magna Carta, for Hume, could not be what it had been for Coke or Petyt—the culmination of the myth of the confirmations going back to the Confessor's time and perhaps before that—what could it represent in the history of the English constitution? In the appendix on "The Feudal and Anglo-Norman Government and Manners," which followed immediately Hume's account of King John's reign, he noted that the Great Charter, in which the king conceded that there was law of the land which even he had to obey,

gave rise, by degrees, to a new species of gevernment, and

38 *Ibid.:* **2:** p. 78.

introduced some order and justice into the administration.
The ensuing scenes of our history are therefore somewhat
different from the preceding . . . And thus the establishment
of the Great Charter, without seeming anywise to innovate in
the distribution of political power, became a kind of epoch in
the constitution.[39]

Hume did not mean that Magna Carta was the beginning of
English liberty: it rather signaled the beginning of a new type
of baronial despotism which only the Tudors could reverse.
It also was a change, an innovation, in the same sense that the
bold demands of the 1620's amounted to a revolution in the
constitution. Hume's understanding of Magna Carta meant
that the Whig interpretation of the constitutional struggle of
the seventeenth century consisted of a double falsification:
the parliamentarians of the England of the early Stuarts were
wrong to use the precedent of the thirteenth century, a time
when Parliament in the modern sense scarcely existed; they
were also wrong in interpreting Magna Carta as a reaffirmation of the ancient constitution, thereby underestimating the
impact of the Conquest and the introduction of the feudal
law.

Having taken a stand on the composition of the
Witenagemot, the impact of the Conquest and subsequent
introduction of feudal law, and the meaning of Magna Carta,
there remained only one disputed issue for Hume to dissect
in his medieval volumes—the origin of the Commons. He
insisted that the Commons played no more of a role in
Anglo-Norman, than it had in Anglo-Saxon, England. Arch-
bishops, and lesser clerical figures, were part of the
Anglo-Norman Great Council as were the barons. The role
of the barons in governing the nation had in fact been en-
hanced by the introduction of feudalism; "they were the
most honorable members of the state, and had a *right* to be
consulted in all public deliberations: They were the immediate vassals of the crown, and owed as a *service* their atten-
dance in the court of their supreme lord." But the Commons,
the representatives of the counties and boroughs, "were no
part of the great council, till some ages after the Conquest . . .
the military tenants alone of the crown composed that supreme legislative assembly." Agreement on this issue, he

---

[39] *Ibid.*, pp. 141-142.

remarked slyly, had been rendered impossible by the stubborn bias of the "ruling party"; he therefore permitted himself to pursue the matter. The need and the desire to debunk the claims of Whigs roused him to amend his text substantially—one of the few times he made any revisions at all in the subsequent editions of the medieval volumes. In the final edition he bolstered his original case concerning the role of the Commons for this period:

> If in the long period of 200 years, which elapsed between the Conquest and the latter end of Henry III and which abounded in factions, revolutions, and convulsions of all kinds, the house of commons never performed a single legislative act, so considerable as to be once mentioned by any of the numerous historians of that age, they must have been totally insignificant.

He then turned to Magna Carta for support. That singularly important document

> provides that no scutage or aid should be imposed, either on the land or towns, but by consent of the great council; and for more security, it enumerates the persons entitled to a seat in that assembly, the prelates and immediate tenants of the crown, without any mention of the commons. An authority so full, so certain, and explicit, that nothing but the zeal of party could ever have procured credit to any contrary hypothesis.[40]

During the reign of Henry III, baronial power was on the ascendant, a trend which in Hume's opinion continued until the arrival of the Tudors. This reign also marked the beginning, however slight, of the influence of the house of Commons. Given the character of Henry III, his youthful accession, his foreign alliances, and the presence of able baronial leaders who wanted to enforce their Great Charter, it is hardly surprising that this reign witnessed the origin of a rudimentary form of parliament. Nor should we be surprised that Hume portrayed this king's trouble with the barons in a manner that made the barons appear as aggressors. The barons accused Henry of having violated Magna Carta, but Hume saw the conflict in a different light: "I reckon not among the violations of the Great Charter some arbitrary exertions of prerogative to which Henry's necessities pushed him, and which, without producing any discon-

---

[40] *Ibid.*, pp. 115-120.

tent, were uniformly continued by all his successors, till the
last century."⁴¹ Even here—in the midst of discussing the
history of the thirteenth century—Hume could not let pass
the opportunity of implicitly shoring up his defense of James
I.

Henry had neither the ability nor the resources to overawe
the barons, and for the first time in English history the
sovereign was forced to compromise with a body which was
becoming known as Parliament. In 1258 the king submitted
to the Provisions of Oxford, by which, Hume thought, "the
monarchy was totally subverted."⁴² There was indeed a pro-
vision for a veto over the king's decisions by a Council of
Fifteen, which was comprised of a baronial majority. For a
while it appeared as though the king were the prisoner of
Lord Edward, his son, and of Simon de Montfort, his
brother-in-law. Edward's fear of Simon's popularity ended
their alliance, and Simon was eventually defeated by Edward
in the king's name, but not before Simon had summoned a
parliament in 1265, where he had hoped to gain adherents
among the gentry. To achieve this goal, two knights from
each shire and two burgesses attended Parliament to represent the towns. The shires and boroughs were thus represented together. For Hume, this act signaled the beginning
of the "epoch of the house of commons in England."⁴³ There
was nothing that exceptional in Hume's observation: the
designation of 49 Henry III as the year the Commons first
met was made by Brady so forcefully that, despite Tyrell's
heated denial of Brady's findings, prudent Whigs like Rapin
were beginning to back off on the issue.⁴⁴

Yet the use Hume made of Brady's Treatise *Of Cities and
Burghs*, which he acknowledged as his source, was quite spe-

----

⁴¹ *Ibid.*, p. 165.
⁴² *Ibid.*, p. 187.
⁴³ *Ibid.*, pp. 210-211.
⁴⁴ Rapin, 1727-1731: **3**: p. 492, merely lists the origin of the House of Commons
as one among many notable events in the reign of Henry III, but no attention is paid
to the significance of this event in the history of the constitution. He deferred
elaborating on the issue because it was "liable to so many disputes." *History of
England* **3**: p. 492. At the turn of the century Tyrell, 1698-1704: **2**: p. cxxvii, refuted
Brady, saying Commons were not new in Henry III's reign "since no historian of the
time referred to them as an innovation."

Hume later wrote that 1295 rather than 1265 was the true beginning of the
Commons, because they then began to meet regularly. Hume, 1778: **2**: p. 272. He
learned this from Brady too. Brady, 1690: pp. 24-25.

cial. Although both historians recognized the late thirteenth-century origin of the Commons, Hume in particular was anxious to stress that the Commons did not then enjoy the prestige or power it came to have in the seventeenth century. Elaborating on Brady, Hume noted that the Commons "were still below the rank of legislators. Their petitions, though they received a verbal assent from the throne, were only the rudiments of laws."[45] Hume then added to what he had learned from Brady. This time the evidence was drawn from Cotton's abridgment of the parliamentary statutes in a footnote to the 1770 edition of the *History:*

> Throughout the reign of Edward I the assent of commons is not once expressed in any of the enacting clauses; nor in the reigns ensuing, till 9 Edward III, nor in any of the enacting clauses of 16 Richard II, nay even so low as Henry VI from the beginning till the 8th of his reign, the assent of the commons is not once expressed in an enacting clause. . . . The commons were so little accustomed to transact public business, that they had no speaker till after the parliament of 6th Edward III.[46]

In the 1770 edition of the *History,* Hume also expanded his argument concerning the origin and nature of the early Commons by using Brady. The case for the antiquity of the Commons was based in part on the petition of the borough of St. Albans, which predated the forty-ninth year of Henry III's reign, but he pointed out that this petition contained falsehoods.[47] St. Albans

> never held of the crown till after the dissolution of the monasteries. But the assurance of these petitioners is remarkable. They wanted to shake off the authority of their abbot, and to hold of the king; but were unwilling to pay any services even to the crown: Upon which they framed this idle petition, which later writers have made the foundation of so many inferences and conclusions.

The so-called antiquity of the Commons was based on this type of spurious evidence. There was authentic evidence for the exact dating of the Commons, the kind Hume borrowed from Brady. But even if it is agreed that the Commons had

---

[45] Hume, 1778: **2:** p. 276.

[46] *Ibid.*, p. 506.

[47] Hume derives this piece of information from Brady's discussion of the petition of St. Albans. Brady, 1684: pp. 37-39.

their beginning in the late thirteenth century, their existence
then was not a valid premise for maintaining that they were
always the palladium of English liberty. Hume asked his
readers to be more historical-minded about the matter than
were some of the Whig historians.

> We are not to imagine, because the house of commons have
> since become of great importance, that the first summoning of
> them would form any remarkable and striking epoch, and
> generally known to the people even seventy or eighty years
> after. So ignorant were the generality of men in that age, that
> country burgesses would readily imagine an innovation, seem-
> ingly so little material, to have existed from time immemorial,
> because it was beyond their own memory, and perhaps that of
> their fathers.[48]

The slur must have been directed not so much at the ignorant men of a distant age, but at the lawyers and pseudo-
historians of a time when they could have known better.

Although for most of Hume's readers the death of Richard III marked only the end of the medieval volumes, it
was, for their author, the end of a six-volume undertaking,
which had been his chief intellectual activity for ten years.
Unlike Gibbon, Hume did not record his feelings at the
moment when he had to concede that the great work was
indeed concluded, but his sense of loss at that time must have
approached that of the historian whom posterity has hon-
ored so much more than the "Tacitus of Scotland." As we
know, Hume, until the last year of his life, maintained an
active interest in editing and improving the work which was
bringing him the fame and fortune he felt he had been
cheated of ever since his *Treatise,* which posterity does indeed
revere, "fell deadborn from the press."

Instead of a memoir inscribing the moment of completion
of the *History,* Hume left a brief epilogue to the medieval
volumes in which he summarized his interpretation of that
period which he believed was so uncivilized in contrast to his
own. At this preeminent place in the *History,* Hume stressed
that throughout the medieval period "the balance of power
has extremely shifted among the several orders of the state;
and this fabric [the constitution] has experienced the same
mutability that has attended all human institutions." His au-

---

[48] Hume, 1778: **2:** pp. 508-509.

dience was told that it was not until their own time, that is, the period since the Glorious Revolution, that the people were able to "erect a regular and equitable plan of liberty." They learned that throughout the "successive alterations" which characterized the actual history of the constitution,

the only rule of government which is intelligible or carries any authority with it, is the established practice of the age, and the maxims of administration which are at that time prevalent and universally attended to. Those who, from a pretended respect to antiquity, appeal at every turn to an original plan of the constitution, only to cover their turbulent spirit and their private ambition under the appearance of venerable forms; and whatever period they pitch on for their model, they may still be carried back to a more ancient period, where they will find the measures of power entirely different, and where every circumstance, by reason of the greater barbarity of the times, will appear still less worthy of imitation.[49]

To Hume the Whig notion of an ancient constitution was dangerous as well as incorrect. By appealing to a mythical past the factious party was in Hume's view willing to challenge irresponsibly established government.

Hume's objections to the Whig interpretation extended beyond history and politics. The idea of an ancient constitution growing steadily and peacefully toward a rational culmination of the realization of liberty was to him a psychological impossibility. The rhythm of medieval history was not unlike the "flux and reflux" of polytheism and theism which he had described in *The Natural History of Religion.* "It is remarkable, that the principles of religion have a kind of flux and reflux in the human mind, and that men have a natural tendency to rise from idolatry to theism, and to sink again from theism to idolatry."[50] Whether monotheism or polytheism took hold depended on several factors, one of them being the ability of a clever priest to promote his god over all the others. During the Middle Ages, the situation was similar with regard to the character of governments: depending on the power of the prince, the nobility or the people were subjected to varying degrees of authority. But no matter who prevailed at a particular moment in the history of those turbulent times, one

---

[49] *Ibid.* **3:** pp. 304-306.
[50] Hume, 1778: **4:** p. 334.

thing was beyond doubt: there was no regular, steady growth
of liberty in the natural *History of England* any more than
there was a steady movement toward or away from
monotheism in the *Natural History of Religion.* Hume never
believed that institutions of human creation were capable of
regular, rational development, and he saw no reason to
exempt the English constitution. In the 1762 edition of the
History he added an apposite observation: "The English Constitution, like all others, has been in a state of continual
fluctuation."[51] To the author of the *Treatise* it was passion,
not reason, that governed human behavior.

As the author of the *Treatise,* Hume saw other opportunities in writing a history of the Middle Ages besides
exposing Whig mythology. His favorite part of the *Treatise*
was the essay "On Miracles," but he declined from publishing
it as part of his first great work, because it so cleverly
ridiculed Christian doctrine by maintaining that miracles
violated what Hume called "the ultimate standard, by which
we determine all disputes . . . experience and observation."[52]
When he became a historian, Hume was able to employ his
empirical and skeptical epistemology freely, and he used the
period most shrouded in superstition and miracles to apply
his technique. The account of Joan of Arc is the most obvious
case in point.

There was no denying the fact that Joan's courage and
leadership were responsible for the French victory at
Orléans, but how could a secular historian explain her visions
and her divine inspiration?

> Joan, inflamed by the general sentiment, was seized with a wild
> desire of bringing relief to her sovereign in his present dis-
> tresses. Her unexperienced mind, working day and night on
> this favorite object, mistook the impulses of passion for heav-
> enly inspirations; and she fancied that she saw visions, and

---

[51] Hume, 1778: **5:** p. 452.

[52] Hume, 1778: **4:** p. 91. Hume had intended this essay to be part of the *Treatise,*
but regretfully deferred printing it until the *Enquiry.* He informed Henry Home of
his decision in terms that reveal his own fondness for this piece. "I am at present
castrating my work, that is, cutting off its nobler parts; that is, endeavouring it shall
give as little offense as possible, before which I could not pretend to put it into the
Doctor's [Joseph Butler, Bishop of Bristol] hands. This is a piece of cowardice, for
which I blame myself, though I believe none of my friends will blame me." Hume,
1932: **1:** p. 25.

heard voices, exhorting her to re-establish the throne of France, and to expel the foreign invaders.[53]

What the credulous had accepted as miraculous, the skeptical could explain as the fancy of an overzealous imagination. Hume had offered the same type of explanation of miraculous behavior in the essay "On Miracles," by showing that behind many fabulous tales there were the exaggerations and lies that the best of men are apt to tell when their love of the extraordinary so inclines them.[54] The philosophe, in addition to criticizing the Whigs' mythical beliefs, was able to help secularize the history of the Middle Ages.

---

[53] Hume, 1778: **3:** p. 142.
[54] Hume, 1882: **4:** pp. 95-97.

Conclusion:
The Achievement, Personal and Professional

The Personal Achievement

The *Annual Register* issued the following notice of the publication of Hume's *History* in 1761:

> Our writers had commonly so ill succeeded in history, the Italians, and even the French, had so long continued our acknowledged superiors, that it was almost feared that the British genius, which had so happily displayed itself in every other kind of writing, and gained the prize in most, yet could not enter in this. The historical work Mr. Hume has published discharged our country from this opprobrium.[1]

Had Hume written the notice himself, he could not have done better. It is uncanny that the reviewer reconstructed the need for history written by a native in virtually the same manner as Hume did when he first wrote to Adam Smith in January, 1753, declaring that there was no post of honor in the English Parnassus more vacant than that of history. That Hume had achieved the recognition and the money, or more significantly the independence that money could offer, is indicated in a number of ways, beyond the formal notice in the *Annual Register*. His publishers consented to four reprintings in his lifetime, and each of the reprintings contained at least some revisions which only a popular seller could justify. Hume received tributes from Gibbon and Voltaire. Gibbon maintained that Hume's encouragement of his own work "overpaid the labor of ten years,"[2] while Voltaire, rather lavishly, called Hume's *History* "perhaps the best written in any language."[3]

Recognition came not only from the greats, who, secure in their own reputations, could afford to be magnanimous.

---

[1] *Annual Register or a View of the History, Politics and Literature for the Year 1761:* **4:** (1761): p. 301.

[2] Gibbon, 1961: p. 175. Gibbon is not overstating the case—as a young man he had thought so highly of Hume that at the latter's advice, he abandoned a history of Germany. *Calendar of Hume MSS* **4:** p. 73.

[3] Voltaire, 1877-1885: **25:** p. 169.

James Boswell, master of the art of borrowing the luster of luminaries, thought a good knowledge of Hume's *History* an important aid in his program for self-improvement and social advancement. Under the entry for January 29, 1763, in his *London Journal,* James Boswell recorded: "I put down mere trifles. I have now one great satisfaction, which is reading Hume's *History.* It entertains and instructs me. It elevates my mind and excites noble feelings of every kind."[4] According to a memorandum included in his remarks describing his day's activities of December 31, 1762, Boswell had been studying the *History* carefully, and was willing to defer his other pleasures to enhance his familiarity with that work. "Dress," he wrote, "then breakfast and be denied. Then journal and Hume, busy till three. Then Louisa; be warm and press home, and talk gently and Digges-like. Acquire an easy dignity and black liveliness of behavior like him. Learn, as Sheridan said, to speak slow and softly."[5] What better way for a young Scotsman on the move in London to impress the literati than by mastering the fashionable history of another Scotsman?

Of course not all reaction to Hume's *History* in Britain was favorable. By the mid-1760's Mrs. Macaulay was busy writing her refutation, and she was merely beginning a task that became central to nineteenth-century Whig historians. Thomas Babington Macaulay hated Hume because of the *History.* In what has been called "perhaps the most severe criticism ever passed by one historian on another,"[6] Macaulay enlisted all his rhetorical talents when he assessed Hume as a historian in the *Edinburgh Review:*

> Hume, without positively asserting much more than he can prove, gives prominence to all the circumstances which support his case. He glides lightly over those which are unfavourable to it. His own witnesses are applauded and encouraged; the statements which seem to throw discredit on them are controverted; the contradictions into which they fall are explained away; a clear and connected abstract of their evidence is given. Everything that is offered on the other side is scrutinized with the utmost severity; every suspicious circumstance is a ground for comment and invective; what cannot be

---

[4] Boswell, 1950: p. 173.
[5] *Ibid.,* p. 113.
[6] Black, 1926: pp. 92-93.

denied is extenuated or passed by without notice. Concessions even are sometimes made; but this insidious candour only increases the effect of this vast mass of sophistry.[7]

George Brodie, in his *History of the British Empire, from the Accession of Charles I to the Restoration* (Edinburgh, 1822), openly declared that it was the "celebrity of Mr. Hume's work" that prompted him to come to the rescue of English historiography, which had suffered because it was "morally impossible" for Hume to have written a true history on the basis of documents available to him.[8] Brodie maintained that Hume's understanding of the history of the English constitution was incorrect (besides being detrimental to the Whig interpretation).

> How erroneous, therefore, is the estimate taken by Mr. Hume of English liberty in former times! He inculcates the notion that the English enjoyed no more freedom than the inhabitants of France and other continental states; and that they were not themselves sensible to any superior privileges. But, had he investigated the matter more deeply, he would have discovered a marked distinction in the respective governments, as well as of its being acknowledged in the strongest terms by foreigners, and fully appreciated by the people themselves.[9]

Henry Hallam, in *The Constitutional History of England from the Accession of Henry VII to the Death of George II* (London, 1865), reproached Hume for having made a comparison of the Tudor monarchy and the despotism of Turkey.[10] In the *Edinburgh Review*, the critic of Charles James Fox's history remarked that Hume "should have sided with the Tudors and the Stuarts against the people, seems inconsistent with all the traits of good character."[11] And, although Gardiner did not take on Hume directly, he did deny Hume's thesis when he insisted that there was a tradition of liberty endemic in the English people, "handed down from father to son from the most ancient times."[12]

Recognition was evidenced not only by formal refutation on the part of historians; it is well attested to by the more than

---

[7] *Edinburgh Review* 29 (October, 1851): pp. 359-360.
[8] George Brodie, 1866: 3: pp. vi-viii.
[9] *Ibid.* 1: p. 6.
[10] Hallam, 1865: 1: p. 227.
[11] *Edinburgh Review* 12 (July, 1808): p. 276.
[12] Gardiner, 1884: 6: p. 120.

two dozen official printings of Hume's *History* in the century after his death, listed in the British Museum Catalogue, and this tally does not include the numerous pirated editions which circulated free from British copyright constraints in Dublin, New York, and Philadelphia. In addition to the complete reprintings, the *History* was condensed for the lazy by the same good Samaritan who later digested Gibbon's history, continued for the curious by Smollett, and Christianized for the young and impressionable. Schoolboys had *The Student's Hume* (London, 1859), those interested in economy had Parsons's "Genuine Pocket Edition" (London, 1793), and families had Hume's *History of England*, "Revised for Family Use, with such omissions and Alterations as may render it Salutary to the Young, and Unexceptionable to the Christian (London, 1816)." No wonder then that the italicized rubric under the entry "David Hume" in the libraries of England and Scotland reads *historian.*

During his own lifetime, Hume did so well by the *History* that not only did the memory of earlier failure seem to disappear, he remained immune to Strahan's flattering attempts to engage him in writing a continuation. Strahan's accolades to Hume as the greatest historian in the eighteenth century, as well as his offer of a generous advance against future royalties, fell on deaf ears: "I must decline not only this offer, but all others of a literary nature for four reasons: Because I'm too old, too fat, too lazy, and too rich."[13] What a difference from the Hume who had to bicker over an unpaid salary from the family of a mad nobleman! The craft of history had not only made Hume rich and independent; it lifted him from provincial obscurity to international prominence. By 1770 both Hume and Scotland (or at least Edinburgh) were central to the European Enlightenment. At that time Hume proclaimed the Enlightenment to be the "historical Age" and Scotland "the historical Nation."[14] It was an immodest claim, but to judge by contemporary opinion, it rang true.

It was not at home in Scotland or in London that Hume achieved his greatest recognition as a historian. In 1763 Hume accompanied Lord Hertford, Britain's first ambassador to France since the outbreak of the Seven Years' War,

---

[13] *Calendar of Hume MSS* **7**: p. 63.
[14] Hume, 1932: **2**: p. 366.

to Paris. Hume was delighted to have been selected as Hertford's private secretary. Although it remains a mystery how he was chosen for the job, the appointment afforded him the chance to get away from Scotland soon after Lord Bute had made Robinson historiographer royal for Scotland—a choice that must have hurt Hume—despite his admiration for Robertson. Moreover, the new position meant that Hume could visit the country where his history of the Stuarts had already been translated and admired. Hume's biographer calls this period of Hume's life "The Adulation of France,"[15] and the wording does not seem extravagant. What is most instructive for us is that most of that adulation was stimulated by the *History*.

Even before leaving with Hertford, the Comtesse de Boufflers informed Hume in what high esteem she held him because of his "histoire de la Maison de Stuard."[16] Hume was not in France long before he had ample reason to believe that Mme de Boufflers's opinion was typical. After three days in Paris, he received a flattering tribute from Mme de Pompadour,[17] and shortly thereafter the dauphin's family at Versailles received him. He decided to write to Robertson (who had the pleasure of a good pension from Bute), describing his reception:

> Do you ask me about my Course of Life? I can only say, that I eat nothing but Ambrosia, drink nothing but Nectar, breathe nothing but Incense, and tread on nothing but Flowers. Every Man I meet, and still more every Lady, wou'd think they were wanting in the most indispensable Duty, if they did not make to me a long & elaborate Harangue in my Praise. What happened last Week, when I had the Honour of being presented to the Dauphin's Children at Versailles, is one of the most curious Scenes I have yet pass'd thro. The Duc de Berry, the eldest, a boy of ten Years old, stept forth, and told me, how many Friends & Admirers I had in this Country, and that he reckond himself in the Number, from the Pleasure he had received by the reading of many Passages in my Works. When he had finish'd, his Brother, the Count de Provence, who is two Years younger, began his Discourse, and informd me, that I

---

[15] Mossner, 1954: pp. 441-456.

[16] Hume, 1932: **2**: p. 366.

[17] *Ibid.*, p. 407. Hume also noted here that the king himself said nothing, but the courtiers told him not to be upset: "he never says anything to anybody, the first time he sees them." *Ibid.*, p. 408.

had been long & impatiently expected in France; and that he himself expected soon to have great Satisfaction from the reading of my fine History. But what is more curious; when I was carry'd thence to the Count d'Artois who is but five Years of Age, I heard him mumble something, which, tho' he had forgot it in the way, I conjectur'd, from some scatterd Words, to have been also a Panegyric dictated to him.[18]

Thus three future kings of France paid their respects to the visiting historian. The tribute paid by the ten-year-old Berry proved prophetic: as King Louis XVI he developed an obsessive interest in Hume's portrayal of the fate of Charles I. When Louis was on trial before the Convention in 1792, Hume's Stuart history became part of the official defense.[19]

Hume's popularity in France was not confined to the royal family or their apologists. Philosophes and *salonnières* who had been cool to Hume as an epistemologist were enthusiastic about Hume the historian. His *History* simply did not pose the same problems as his formal philosophy. As a historian, he did not have to compete with the lingering affection for Descartes, and his atheism did not have to be dealt with directly. D'Alembert told Hume that his *History* was popular in the salons, and Mme d'Epinay referred to him as "the celebrated David Hume, the great historian of England."[20] Hume arrived in France at a perfect time to profit from the Anglomania which had been temporarily attenuated by the Seven Years' War.

Hume was first to acknowledge that his reception in France changed his status in the Republic of Letters. He went from outcast philosopher to renowned historian. He was incredulous. Reflecting on his popularity, he asked Smith: "But can I ever forget, that it is the very same Species, that wou'd scarce show me common Civilities a very few Years ago at Edinburgh, who now receive me with such Applauses at Paris?"[21] A few weeks later he wondered in jest to Adam Ferguson if he would be thrown out of France "à coup des compliments et des louanges."[22] There is no joke without truth and this instance is no exception. History brought

---

[18] Hume, 1954: pp. 74-75.
[19] Bongie, 1965: pp. 126-133.
[20] Mossner, 1954: p. 444.
[21] Hume, 1932: 1: p. 409.
[22] *Ibid.*, p. 410.

Hume the acclaim he had feared, at the age of forty-one, he might never receive. It also became the one medium through which he could express to a wide audience his politics, his affinity for the progressive aspects of the Edinburgh Enlightenment, and his abiding resentment of the Whig oligarchy.

Within Hume's lifetime the history of his country had progressed in directions in which he took personal pride. Improvement was accomplished in the many areas that interested him and the other Edinburgh literati: trade was beginning to flourish; revenue and population were increasing many times over; the University of Edinburgh was beginning to compete with the finest institutions of Holland; and the city itself was transforming under his very eyes. In 1772 the North Bridge was built; it linked the dingy Edinburgh of John Knox to the splendid New Town, which claimed David Hume as one of its first residents. The bridge spanned only a short distance, but its construction gave the literary giants of Britain access to quarters suitable to their genius and to their reputation. Hume was delighted to see the New Town grow and become beautiful. After settling there he wrote to a potential resident, "I charge you not to think of settling in London, till you have first seen our New Town, which exceeds anything you have seen in any part of the world."[23]

Hume's last residence in the New Town was on St. David Street; it was here that he received, less than half a year before his death, the great works of Adam Smith and Edward Gibbon. He happily congratulated them both. He had helped inspire those works, and he knew it—Scotland had improved in nothing so much as in literature and history. The country he had, as a youth, tried to escape to obtain status was now a comfortable place to hear the applause of literate Europe. Despite the half-serious contentions of his admirers, Hume was no saint; he lived to enjoy the knowledge that he, more than anyone else, had made Edinburgh one of the literary capitals of Europe, the rival of London and Paris.

---

[23] *Ibid.* **2:** p. 267.

The Professional Achievement

In describing the transition from the age of antiquarian research and erudite scholarship that distinguished late seventeenth-century England to the age of Enlightenment of the mid-eighteenth century, David C. Douglas has written: "There are few more notable changes in the development of English culture than that which rapidly transformed this climate of opinion so that by the middle of the eighteenth century the leaders of English taste had come to profess almost a hatred of the past, and a disdain for those who explored it."[24] Elsewhere in his excellent study of Restoration historians, Professor Douglas laments "the end of an age" when he notes that during the Enlightenment "earlier motives for inquiry were disdained . . . elegance was rated above research, and interpretation above discovery."[25] He further insists that "an Age of Enlightenment could afford to be ignorant of the centuries which preceded it, and the minute investigation of history became an occupation unworthy of a man of sensibility . . . the fiery zeal of scholars degenerated into a prying devoid of reverence, into mild curiosity destitute of serious purpose."[26] This heavy indictment, coming from a present-day scholar as accomplished as Professor Douglas deserves serious consideration, not in the least because it contains some truth.

That during the Enlightenment there was a decline in the type of antiquarian endeavor to which a Thomas Rymer was willing to devote a lifetime is beyond doubt. It is just as undeniable (and unfortunate) that there was a decline in the editing of medieval texts. The learned group of worshipful men who are central to Professor Douglas's study did not live into a secular age when historians asked different questions of the past and sought answers in very irreverent and sometimes slipshod ways.

The example of Hume reveals both some of the strengths and weaknesses of Enlightenment historiography. When Hume started on the first of his Stuart volumes he had one idea and a great deal of frustrated energy. He had no notion

---

[24] Douglas, 1951: p. 273.
[25] *Ibid.*, pp. 27-28.
[26] *Ibid.*, pp. 274-275.

where his historical insight would lead him; he knew only
that the Whigs were wrong to present James I as the great
subverter of English liberty. He used every bit of evidence he
could find to document his case, but he did not even acknowledge his sources in the first edition. We know that he
said he was following the example of Machiavelli and other
moderns who omitted their sources, but this justification
appears rather lame—many moderns carefully listed their
references. It seems more likely that his casual attitude may
be explained by the fact that he was unaware of how involved
he would become in the *History* when he began writing. But
the more he became involved with the task at hand, the more
his interest in the sources grew, and so did his willingness to
credit them. True, he never showed that systematic devotion
to precise references characteristic of seventeenth-century antiquarians, or even eighteenth-century compilers: some of
his aversion to excessive documentation may have been a
reaction to Rapin's inclusion of lengthy documents.[27] As he
approached the career of historian, he quite understandably
demonstrated the sensibility of the essayist—he was more
aware of deficiencies in style than of the necessity for rigorous documentation.

Still, Hume's interest in pursuing the profession of a historian was inspired not by a disinterested devotion to understanding the past, but by his mania for dethroning the Whigs
from their position as *the* historians of England. Almost every
instance of his historical curiosity can be traced back to this
stimulus, whether it was his discovery of James II's memoirs
in Paris, or his use of the work of Brady in the medieval
volumes. The partnership with Robertson in the campaign
against Mary, Queen of Scots, is the single best example of
this type of polemically stimulated scholarship, although, in
this instance, Jacobites rather than Whigs felt the sting of his
vitriolic critique. Enlightenment historiography was almost
always a partisan undertaking, but the partisanship no more
diminished the quality of the achievement of the philosophes
than the struggle to authenticate the antiquity of the true
Church invalidated the work of the Reformation and Coun-
terreformation scholars who did brilliant work in order to

---

[27] See Chapter I, note 40.

discover whose church was the original. Motives change, but history is seldom a dispassionate undertaking.

If we wish to understand Hume's attitude toward his sources as well as his conception of the proper role of the historian, we need to consider his candid remarks on these subjects. While he was writing the Tudor volumes he was inexorably drawn into a number of controversies which required his acknowledgement of sources. In the case of his attack against Perkin Warbeck, it was with condescending resentment that he had to go beyond More and Bacon to "contemporary evidence . . . so much sought after."[28] But he went after it, even if he believed, as his tone suggested, that interest in primary documentation was something of a fad. On the other hand, he gladly out-researched Robertson on the question of the Queen of Scots's guilt. The Stuart volumes were entirely based on the published *Journals* of the Commons and on the widely read works of historians such as Clarendon, Walker, or Whitlock. While the Tudor volumes were still almost completely based on printed parliamentary statutes, and on the histories of Polydore Virgil, John Camden, and John Strype, and even more on the monumental *Foedera* of Thomas Rymer, sporadic attention was paid to manuscript evidence and to the reliability of conflicting contemporary accounts.

Hume did not share the antiquarian ambition of discovering, deciphering, collecting, and publishing original manuscripts. Professor Douglas is right in this regard. The type of scholarship which graced Elizabethan and Jacobean culture in the works of Robert Cotton, Humphrey Wanley, and Thomas Hearne did not flourish in the age of Enlightenment, but interest in history did not end. Historians during the Enlightenment addressed a wider audience than their antiquarian predecessors (or many of their successors), and they tended to write histories that covered longer periods of time or greater portions of the Earth than had been the custom. Hume saw his place in the development of historiography quite clearly—he was, he explained to Horace Walpole, a popularizer and a synthesizer. "If no man is to know the English story but by perusing all those monuments, which remain of it," Hume contended,

[28] Hume, 1778: **3:** p. 456.

few will be able to attain that useful and agreeable erudition. The original books, which instruct us in the reign of Q. Elizabeth alone, would require six months reading at the rate of ten hours a day; and most people, even after taking this pains, wou'd attain but a very confus'd idea of the transactions of that period. But what must foreigners do to get some notion of our history? What must posterity, after these monuments have farther multiply'd upon us? What must far the greatest part of ourselves, who have neither leisure nor inclination for such a laborious and disagreeable study?[29]

Hume intended to use the work of antiquarians to give his audience an accessible history. It was his job to glean from the monuments of the past what he thought was useful for his readers to know. Like Bolingbroke he believed in the didactic function of history—all the more reason to improve on Rapin's prolixity. When the narrative is smooth and concise the lessons of history are more easily assimilated.

Hume envisaged an audience that did not have the time to read more than the essentials: knowledge was on the increase and so was commerce. The world of the eighteenth century was expanding in all directions; yet historians did not specialize as a result. Hume revealed much when he wrote to John Douglas about the latter's plans to publish memoirs of the Earl of Clarendon.

Do you intend to publish all Clarendon's Papers, or only the more material ones? I should think the last Method more satisfying to everybody except Historians: And even they would not be displeased that you spare them a great deal of superfluous Reading. Had Thurloe's Papers been reduc'd to one Volume, they had been more useful as well as more entertaining.[30]

Even the historian was impatient, and unwilling to ask very much more of himself than of his readers.

Not only was specialization inappropriate for the Enlightenment historian; so were the constraints that would be placed on the profession by nineteenth-century historicists. Hume hailed the invention of the printing press because it gave the historian the "power of selecting, as well as adorning

---

[29] Hume, 1932: 1: p. 285.
[30] Ibid., p. 334.

the facts which he relates."[31] The critical methods and professional institutions of the nineteenth century, which we
must distinguish as "the imperatives of modern scholarship,"[32] were simply not present in Hume's time, and this
permitted him a sense of freedom which is no longer part of
the historians' *métier*. Hume was a great ornament of that age
of gentlemen-historians who could write without institutional
support and the watchful eye of specialists. It was not yet
the time of Ranke or his disciples.

It is clear enough what Hume did not do. We must ask the
more important question of what his precise contribution to
the history of history was, coming as it did after an-
tiquarianism and before professionalization. Hume's brand
of scholarship yielded a new synthesis in the development of
historiography. By borrowing from the work of a philological expert like Brady and placing it in the context of narrative history, Hume was able to give the reading public in
England the first national history that was both critical and
readable.

Brady was an extraordinary scholar, but he was not a
historian in the modern sense of the term. His major contribution to British historiography was his ability to show that
Whig interpretation was invalid because it rested on the
legalistic notion of precedents. The Whigs evolved a type of
argument that was actually teleological—attempting to justify
a "reassertion" of rights, they examined the past in order to
find precedents for those rights. Such a process may be
appropriate for lawyers, who must defend changes in the
constitution by arguing that they are not ruptures with tradition, but it is not suitable to the historian, who is obliged to
acknowledge changes and discontinuities when he sees them.
Brady explained that Cotton, Selden, and Coke were wrong
about the governance of the early boroughs because they
failed to explore what the various terms meant in the context
of the times they were writing about. They saw the word
"burgh" and thought that it had the same significance in
Saxon England as it did in their own seventeenth century.
This procedure was comprehensible enough coming from
lawyers defending their aggressive program by arguing from

---

[31] Hume, 1778: **3:** p. 407.
[32] Higham, 1965: p. 320.

precedent, but it was also wrong. Using the techniques of comparative philology, Brady was able to pinpoint the fallacy of the Whig argument. He was indefatigable. He consulted Salic glossaries, traced the origins of words, such as Burgh, in Saxon dictionaries, produced Norman parliament writs—all in the effort to prove that the Whig lawyers were not really historians because they did not, he insisted, "truly understand the meaning of the words" they so freely employed.[33]

Indispensable though Brady's work was to correcting the Whig interpretation, it was not history. Professor Pocock, among the first to recognize Brady's accomplishments, concedes that

> in Brady we have followed to a high degree of development a particular technique of historical criticism that arose in the study of English law and produced in him vigorous and subtle historical insight; but we are compelled at the last to admit that he had no notion of how to combine the reconstruction of institutions with the narrative of men's deeds—how to combine legal antiquarianism with history as a literary art. To this extent, and viewing the matter from this standpoint, we are still in the prehistory, or in a primitive age of modern historiography.[34]

Brady's "histories" are indeed for the most part linguistic exercises; they are excellent and learned works of reference but they cannot be read as narrative history. Hume did not do the type of philological deciphering and patient analysis of ancient legal documents that enabled Brady to understand feudalism, but he neither had to do what was already done, or pretend to do that kind of work. Rather he perceived the significance of Brady's research once he realized they were on the same side of the polemical fence, and then proceeded to integrate Brady's findings into a history that told the story of English history to an audience Brady would never have reached.

Hume's achievement in synthesizing and popularizing Brady's work is too often overlooked. Pocock has written that

> the heirs of Spelman died beaten and broken men, perishing among the spears of triumphant Whiggery. With their defeat ended the first serious attempt to give feudalism its proper

---

[33] Brady, 1690: p. 62.
[34] Pocock, 1967: pp. 225-226.

place in English history, and there was not another until the
nineteenth century, when the task was successfully accomplished by historians whom we feel to be still our contemporaries. The failure of Brady to convince his countrymen
undeniably marked a setback for the course of English historiography.[35]

Brady's career did end unhappily: when he surrendered the
key to the Tower records to Petyt, he was cut off from a
brilliant course of study at a time when his mind was still
keen. But the writing of critical history did not have to wait
for Maitland and Stubbs. Between Brady and the late
nineteenth-century historians stands Hume, not as the
originator of the critical approach but as a popularizer of it.
At the height of the Whig heyday, Hume reintroduced
Brady and made him more widely appreciated than he had
been in his own time.

Professor Douglas is to be credited with having brought to
our attention the enormous achievement of Sir Robert Brady
in medieval studies, but he is also responsible for depreciat-
ing the reputation of at least one historian who relied on
Brady's work in the eighteenth century. Douglas has written:

> Brady was a master of record learning, and his achievement in
> historical scholarship has been regrettably belittled by the faint
> praise of those who were content silently to profit by his erudi-
> tion while condemning his political opinions. . . . What requires
> more emphatic statement is that his learned conclusions are
> embodied in many standard works of a later date which omit to
> state the source from which they are derived.

He then adds as a footnote to this contention: "Hume, for
example, was much indebted to Brady."[36] Yet Hume's debt
to Brady is openly acknowledged all through the pages of the
medieval volumes of the *History*. Soon after the publication of
the entire *History of England*, Hume assured his publisher:

---

[35] *Ibid.*, p. 228. Pocock has recently stated that some of his observations in the
concluding chapter of the *Ancient Constitution* are replaced by chapters XIII and
XIV of the *Machiavellian Moment*. Pocock, 1976: p. 102n. In these chapters Pocock
gives full recognition to the challenges made to ancient constitutionalism in the
eighteenth century, especially during the paper war against Walpole. But as I have
hoped to demonstrate, ancient constitutionalism and an uncritical view of feudalism
were still in vogue when Hume set out to attack these notions, despite the exchange
between the *London Journal* and Bolingbroke's *Craftsman*.

[36] Douglas, 1951: p. 125.

There is not a Quotation that I did not see with my own Eyes, except two or three at most, which I took from Tyrrel or Brady because I had not the Books refer'd to. That there is no Mistake in such Number of References, would be rash or even absurd to affirm: That the Printer also has not sometimes made Mistakes in the name of the Author or in the Number of the Page quoted, is what I dare not aver: For I only compared the Sheet now & then with my Manuscript, and was contented to be as correct as possible in the Text. I knew that these Mistakes could neither be frequent nor material. But if People, finding a few here & there, point them out, and give them as a Specimen of the whole, I know no remedy for this Malice, but to allow them to go on. Men of Candour will judge otherwise without Scrutiny: and Men of Diligence & Industry will find that the Case is otherwise upon Scrutiny.[37]

It is hoped that our discussion of Hume's *History* has demonstrated his industry, if not his precise scrutiny, when it came to borrowing from the great works of his predecessors, his willingness to praise them, and his implicit wish to be placed in their tradition.

Hume's reputation as a professional historian has also suffered because he once wrote, "Mankind are so much the same, in all times and places, that history informs us of nothing new or strange in this particular."[38] Some critics have taken this to mean that to Hume (and they generally include the other Enlightenment historians) the past was a monochrome of boring events and faceless characters whose only importance was that they somehow all anticipated the great age of reason. J. B. Black, for example, helped spread the notion that Hume treated characters as types, that to him they were nothing more than a series of repeating decimals.[39] Even more widely respected students of historiography, such as R. G. Collingwood, have agreed. In addition to asserting that Hume's *History* was "a slight and sketchy piece of work,"[40] Collingwood maintained that Hume conceived of human nature "as something static and permanent."[41] George Sabine has written that Hume "missed the essentially historical point of view, because he was thus led to

---

[37] Hume, 1932: **1:** p. 355.
[38] Hume, 1882: **4:** p. 68.
[39] Black, 1926: pp. 100-101.
[40] Collingwood, 1946: p. 78.
[41] *Ibid.*, p. 82.

neglect the unique and individual aspects of historical events and persons."[42] Carl Becker, responsible for making so many misconceptions of the Enlightenment popular, insisted that this sentence from the *Enquiry* was "the sum and substance"[43] of Hume's philosophy of history. It was logical for Becker to conclude that Hume's history was a "dull and colorless chronicle of events."[44]

It is difficult to imagine that these men ever divorced themselves from the Romantics' condemnation of Enlightenment history long enough to read the outstanding historical works of the eighteenth century. What Hume meant by his statement in the *Enquiry* was that human nature had the same potential for learning and enlightenment through the ages, and that this potential could either be cultivated and developed in rational pursuits or destroyed by war, fanaticism, and stupidity. Hume also believed that custom, habit, and experience governed human behavior; that there was no such animal as rational man in the abstract; that human institutions were in a constant state of flux. This conviction underlay his understanding of the history of the English constitution and helped make his critique of the Whig interpretation possible. Men's behavior, values, and morals changed all the time. Hume was much more of a relativist than most critics have maintained. In A *Dialogue,* published in 1751, he contrasted the morality of ancient Greece with that of modern Europe and pronounced in almost a historicist vein that Greeks and Romans should not be judged by the customs of English common law.[45]

Rather than make his history flat or sketchy, Hume's philosophy of human nature made it possible for his history to be filled with characters as divergent and as interestingly portrayed as Joan of Arc and Thomas More. In Voltaire's *Dictionnaire philosophique,* the interlocutors are Chinese and Arabic, as well as Western European. They come from vastly different cultures and their experiences vary immensely; but it is their capacity to agree on common sense morality that unites them. Their common moral sense, however, does not diminish our curiosity about the variety of cultures that

---

[42] Sabine, 1906: p. 38.
[43] Becker, 1932: p. 95.
[44] *Ibid.,* p. 109.
[45] Hume, 1882: **4:** pp. 289-305.

formed their individual personalities. So it is in Hume's *History*, where we meet a host of characters who reflect the environment of English and European society as it evolved from the early Middle Ages to the eighteenth century. Elsewhere, Hume wrote that, at least so far as cultural history was concerned, "those who consider the periods and revolutions of human kind, as represented in history, are entertained with a spectacle full of pleasure and variety, and see, with surprize, the manners, customs, and opinions of the same species susceptible of such prodigious changes in different periods of time."[46] He admitted that "wars, negotiations, and politics" offered less of an entertaining spectacle,[47] but when critics are choosing quotations to describe Hume's philosophy of history, it might be more just to his historical performance if they chose this one, rather than the isolated and misleading statement from the *Enquiry*. Fortunately, in recent literature, Hume's statement about the uniformity of human nature is being put in more accurate perspective.[48]

One of the most unfortunate aspects of the historicist legacy is its negative assessment of the historians of the Enlightenment. In addition to being an egregiously unhistoricist point of view, it has been immensely influential and incorrect, if understood as uniformly true.[49] Hume, for example, does not judge the political maxims or the social mores of one age by those of another. Not only did he make this point explicitly in *A Dialogue;* the very fabric of the *History of England* is woven with this contention in mind. The Whigs were wrong in point of historical fact; but, more than that, it was anti-historical of them, as Hume continually says, to anticipate in all ages and in all times the origins of the sacred

---

[46] *Ibid.*, **3:** p. 163.

[47] *Ibid.*, p. 164.

[48] Meyer, 1958: p. 55. Meyer makes the well-taken point that Hume's much quoted remark was made before he started writing history, and that "in the course of his historical investigations he had considerably modified his earlier belief in the uniformity of human nature, and we find indications of historical relativism."

S. K. Wertz, 1975: pp. 481-496. Wertz systematically, and to my mind, convincingly, refutes the notion that Hume's understanding of human nature was static. Hume's historical relativism is also discussed in Gay, 1969: **2:** pp. 380-385.

[49] Following the lead of Dilthey, Cassirer detected damaging inconsistency in the historicist view of the eighteenth-century historiography. "Romanticism was historically blind to the generation of its own fathers. It never attempted to judge the Enlightenment by its own standards, and it was unable to view without polemical bias the conception of the historical world which the eighteenth-century has formulated." Cassirer, 1951: p. 198.

plan of liberty. In this sense Hume's polemical work was an altogether positive contribution for the history of history.

Ironically enough, it was Meinecke, admiring Enlightenment historiography only because it somehow prefigured the blossoming of nineteenth-century historicism, who pointed to one of the most attractive qualities of Hume's *History:* "its strong intellectual substructure."[50] It was indeed Hume's ability to argue forcefully and intelligently that made the *History* such a compelling work. Whether Hume's readers agreed with him or hated him because he trenchantly criticized the commonplaces of British historiography so dear to many, none could resist acknowledging that Britain at last had a native historian who could write what Palgrare called, in his article on Hume as a historian over a century ago, "historical literature in the aesthetic sense of the term."[51] The post of historian in the English Parnassus was indeed no longer vacant.

---

[50] Meinecke, 1959: **3:** p. 197.
[51] Palgrave, 1844: p. 540.

Bibliography

I. DAVID HUME

A. *Manuscripts*

1932. *Calendar of Hume MSS in the Possession of the Royal Society of Edinburgh* (6 v., compiled by J. Y. T. Greig and Harold Beynon, Edinburgh).
Historical Memoranda
"Memoranda for my history of England written July, 1745 or 1746. David Hume. James Court, 1751." MS. 732, National Library of Scotland.
"No. 2 Memoranda of Notes and data for my history of England, 1749. David Hume. James Court." MS. 733, National Library of Scotland.
"No. 5. See Miscellaneous Notes, Memoranda and &c for my history of England written during the year 1749. James Court 1759." MS. 734, National Library of Scotland.
"Memoranda and Notes for my history of England made in the year 1749. David Hume, 23 May 1755, At James Court Lawnmarket." MS. HM 12263, Huntington Library.

B. *Printed Works*

1754. *The History of Great Britain, Containing the Reigns of James I and Charles I* (Edinburgh).
1757. *The History of Great Britain, Containing the Commonwealth and Reigns of Charles II and James II* (London).
1759. *The History of England Under the House of Tudor; Comprehending the Reigns of Henry VII, Henry VIII, Edward VI and Mary* (London).
1762. *The History of England from the Invasion of Julius Caesar to the Accession of Henry VII* (2 v., London).
1762, 1763, 1770, 1773, 1778. *The History of England from the Invasion of Julius Caesar to the Revolution in 1688* (8 v., London).
1882. *The Philosophical Works of David Hume* (4 v., edited by T. H. Green and T. H. Grose, London).
1932. *The Letters of David Hume* (2 v., edited by J. Y. T. Gierg, Oxford).
1948. *Dialogues Concerning Natural Religion* (edited by Norman Kemp Smith, New York).
1954. *New Letters of David Hume* (edited by R. Klibansky and E. C. Mossner, Oxford).
1962. "New Hume Letters to Lord Elibank, 1748-1776." Edited by E. C. Mossner. *Texas Studies in Literature and Language* **4**: 3: pp. 442-452.
1967. *A Letter from a Gentleman to his Friend in Edinburgh* (edited by E. C. Mossner and J. V. Price, Edinburgh).

II. OTHER PRIMARY WORKS

A. *Manuscripts*

National Library of Scotland:
Letters Concerning Mary, Queen of Scots. MSS. 35.1.1.

"Minutes and Procedures of the Select Society." MS. 23.1.1.
"Proceedings of the Belles Lettres Society." MS. 23.3.4.
"Minutes of the Faculty of Advocates 1751-1782." MSS.
"Registrar of the Proceedings of the Curators and Keeper of the Library in relation to their Office Beggining Anno 1725." MSS.
"Rules and Orders of the Select Society." MS. 23.1.0.
"Sir J. Stuart's Observations on Hume's History Relative to Q. M. Stuart." MS. 321.68.

B. *Printed Works*

Annual Register or a View of the History, Politics and Literature for the Year 1761 **4** (1761).
ATWOOD, WILLIAM. 1682. *Argumentum Anti-Normanicum or an Argument Proving from Ancient Histories and Records that William made no Absolute Conquest* (London).
BAXTER, JOHN. 1796. *A New and Impartial History of England* (London).
BLACKSTONE, WILLIAM. 1783. *Commentaries on the Laws of England* (6 v., London).
BRADY, ROBERT. 1681. *A Full and Clear Answer to a Book Written by William Petyt, Esq.* (London).
————. 1684. *An Introduction to Old English History* (London).
————. 1685. *A Complete History of England* (2 v., London).
————. 1690. *An Historical Treatise of Cities, and Burghs* (London).
BOLINGBROKE, VISCOUNT (HENRY ST. JOHN). 1841. *The Works of Lord Bolingbroke* (4 v., Philadelphia).
BOSWELL, JAMES. 1934-1950. *Boswell's Life of Johnson, Together with Boswell's Journal of a Tour to the Hebrides and Johnson's Diary of a Journey into North Wales* (edited by George Birkbeck Hill, revised by L. F. Powell, 6 v., Oxford).
————. 1950. *London Journal, 1762-3* (edited by Frederick A. Pottle, New York).
————. 1970. *Boswell in Extremes, 1776-1778* (edited by M. C. Weis and Frederick A. Pottle, New York).
BRODIE, GEORGE. 1866. *A History of the British Empire from the Accession of Charles I to the Restoration* (3 v., London).
CALAMY, EDMUND. 1718. *A Letter to Mr. Archdeacon Echard Upon the Occasion of his History of England* (London).
CARLYLE, ALEXANDER. 1861. *The Autobiography of Alexander Carlyle* (Boston).
CARLYLE, THOMAS. 1904. *On Heroes, Hero-Worship and the Heroic in History* (London).
CARTE, THOMAS. 1747-1750. *A General History of England* (4 v., London).
Critical Review **2** (December, 1756).
DALRYMPLE, SIR JOHN. 1773. *Memoirs of Great Britain and Ireland* (2 v., London).
ECHARD, LAWRENCE. 1707-1718. *The History of England* (2 v., London).
Edinburgh Review **1** (July, 1755); **2** (January, 1756); **12** (July, 1808); **94** (March, 1851).
GIBBON, EDWARD. 1961. *The Autobiography of Edward Gibbon* (edited by Dero A. Saunders, New York).
GODWIN, WILLIAM. 1824. *A History of the Commonwealth from its Commencement to the Restoration of Charles the Second* (4 v., London).
GUTHRIE, WILLIAM. 1750-1751. *The History of England* (3 v., London).
HALLAM, HENRY. 1865. *The Constitutional History of England from the Accession of Henry VII to the Death of George II* (3 v., London).
HERVEY, JOHN. 1734. *Ancient and Modern Liberty Stated and Compar'd* (London).
HYDE, EDWARD, EARL OF CLARENDON. 1888. *History of the Rebellion and Civil Wars in England* (6 v., Oxford).
JEFFERSON, THOMAS. 1944. *Life and Selected Writings* (edited by Adrienne Koch and William Peden, New York).
JOHNSON, SAMUEL. 1905. *Lives of the English Poets* (3 v., edited by G. B. Hill, Oxford).
KNOX, JOHN. 1949. *The History of the Reformation in Scotland* (2 v., edited by William Croft Dickinson, London).

LOCKE, JOHN. 1960. *Two Treatises of Government* (edited by Peter Laslett, Cambridge, 1960).
LYTTLETON, SIR GEORGE. 1764-1771. *History of the Life of Henry II* (5 v., London).
MACCAULAY, CATHERINE GRAHAM. 1763-1768. *The History of England from the Accession of James I to the Elevation of the House of Hanover* (8 v., London).
MCQUEEN, DANIEL. 1756. *Letters on Mr. Hume's History of Great Britain* (Edinburgh).
MILL, JOHN STUART. 1962. *Essays on Politics and Culture* (edited by Gertrude Himmelfarb, New York).
The Monthly Review or Literary Journal 12 (March, 1755).
OLDMIXON, JOHN. 1728. *A Critical History of England* (London).
PERCY, THOMAS. 1770. *The Regulations and Establishment of the Household of Henry Algernon Percy* (London).
PETYT, WILLIAM. 1680. *The Antient Right of the Commons of England Asserted* (London).
RAPIN, THOYRAS PAUL DE. 1724. *Histoire d'Angleterre* (10 v., The Hague).
————. 1726-1731. *The History of England* (15 v., translated by N. Tindal, London).
ROBERTSON, WILLIAM. 1851. *History of Scotland* (2 v., London).
Scots Magazine. March, 1757.
TOWERS, JOHN. 1778. *Observations on Mr. Hume's History of England* (London).
TYRELL, JAMES. 1698-1704. *The General History of England* (3 v., London).
TYTLER, WILLIAM. 1760. *An historical and critical Enquiry . . .* (Edinburgh).
VOLTAIRE (AROUET, FRANÇOIS-MARIE). 1877-1885. *Œuvres complètes* (52 v., edited by Louis Moland, Paris).
————. 1957. *Œuvres historiques* (edited by Rene Pomeau, Paris).
WALKER, CLEMENT. 1648. *History of Independency* (London).
WALPOLE, HORACE. 1965. *Historic Doubts on the Life and Reign of King Richard III: The Great Debate* (edited by Paul Murry Kendall, New York).

III. SECONDARY WORKS

BECKER, CARL. 1932. *The Heavenly City of the Eighteenth-Century Philosophers* (New Haven).
BONGIE, LAWRENCE L. 1965. *David Hume: Prophet of the Counter-Revolution* (Oxford).
BLARK, J. B. 1926. *The Art of History: A Study of Four Great Historians in the Eighteenth Century* (London).
BRAUDY, LEO. 1970. *Narrative Form in History and Fiction: Home, Fielding and Gibbon* (Princeton).
BREDVOLD, LOUIS I. 1956. *The Intellectual Milieu of John Dryden: Studies in Some Aspects of Seventeenth-Century Thought* (Ann Arbor).
BRIGGS, ASA. 1959. *The Making of Modern England, 1783-1867: The Age of Improvement* (London).
BRUMFITT, J. H. 1958. *Voltaire Historian* (Oxford).
BRYSON, GLADYS. 1945. *Man and Society: The Scottish Inquiry of the Eighteenth Century* (Princeton).
BUTTERFIELD, HERBERT. 1945. *The Englishman and His Past* (Cambridge).
————. 1965. *The Whig Interpretation of History* (New York).
BURTON, JOHN HILL. 1846. *The Life and Correspondence of David Hume* (2 v., London).
CASSIRER, ERNST. 1951. *The Philosophy of the Enlightenment* (translated by C. A. Koelln and James P. Pettigrove, Princeton).
COLLINGWOOD, R. G. 1946. *The Idea of History* (London).
DILTHEY, WILHELM. 1959. "Das achtzehnte Jahrhundert und die geschichtliche Welt." *Gesammelte Schriften* 3: pp. 210-268 (Stuttgart).
DOUGLAS, DAVID C. 1951. *English Scholars 1660-1730* (London).
————. 1964. *William the Conqueror: The Impact Upon England* (London).
FIRTH, SIR CHARLES. 1896. "Rapin, Paul Thoyras." *Dictionary of National Biography* 16: pp. 740-743.

FORBES, DUNCAN. 1970. "Introduction." David Hume, *The History of Great Britain* (London).
————. 1976. *Hume's Philosophical Politics* (Cambridge).
FRANKLIN, JULIAN H. 1963. *Jean Bodin and the Sixteenth Century Revolution in the Methodology of Law and History* (New York).
FUSSNER, SMITH F. 1962. *The Historical Revolution: English Historical Writing and Thought 1580-1640* (London).
GARDINER, S. R. 1896. *The History of England from the Accession of James I to the Outbreak of the Civil War (1603-1642)* (10 v., London).
GAY, PETER. 1966. *A Loss of Mastery: Puritan Historians in Colonial America* (Berkeley and Los Angeles).
————. 1965, 1969. *The Enlightenment: An Interpretation* **1**: *The Rise of Modern Paganism;* **2**: *The Science of Freedom* (New York).
————. 1964. *The Party of Humanity: Essays in the French Enlightenment* (New York).
————. 1959. *Voltaire's Politics: The Poet as Realist* (Princeton).
GIARRIZZO, GIUSEPPE. 1962. *David Hume politico e storico* (Milan).
GRAHAM, HENRY. 1901. *Scottish Men of Letters in the Eighteenth Century* (2 v., London).
————. 1928. *The Social Life of Scotland in the Eighteenth Century* (London).
HEXTER, J. H. 1941. *The Reign of King Pym* (Cambridge, Mass.)
HIGHAM, JOHN, LEONARD KRIEGER, and FELIX GILBERT, eds. 1965. *History* (Princeton).
JONES, J. R. 1961. *The First Whigs* (London).
KELLEY, DONALD R. 1970. *Foundations of Modern Historical Scholarship: Language, Law, and History in the French Renaissance* (New York).
KRAMNICK, ISAAC. 1967. "Augustan Politics and English Historiography: The Debate on the English Past, 1730-35." *History and Theory* **6**, 1: pp. 35-67.
————. 1968. *Bolingbroke and His Circle: The Politics of Nostalgia in the Age of Walpole* (Cambridge, Mass.).
LEE, MAURICE, JR. 1965. *The Cabal* (Urbana, Ill.).
MACCAFFREY, WALLACE. 1968. *The Shaping of the Elizabethan Regime* (Princeton).
MCELROY, D. D. 1969. *Scotland's Age of Improvement* (Washington).
MAITLAND, F. W. 1897. *Domesday Book and Beyond* (London).
MEINECKE, FRIEDRICH. 1959. *Werke* **3**: *Die Entstehung des Historismus* (Munich).
MOSSNER, ERNEST C. 1941. "An Apology for David Hume, Historian." *Publ. Mod. Lang. Assn.* **16**: pp. 657-690.
MOSSNER, ERNEST C., and HARRY RANSOM, 1950. "Hume and the 'Conspiracy of the Booksellers'; The Publication and Early Fortunes of the History of England." *Univ. of Texas Studies in English* **29**: pp. 162-182.
————. 1954. *The Life of David Hume* (Austin, Texas).
————. 1941. "Was Hume a Tory Historian? Facts and Reconsiderations." *Jour. History of Ideas* **2**: pp. 225-236.
NEALE, J. E. 1966. *Elizabeth and Her Parliaments, 1559-1581* (New York).
NORTON, DAVID FATE, and RICHARD POPKIN, eds. 1965. *David Hume: Philosophical Historian* (Indianapolis).
NOTESTEIN, WALLACE. 1966. "The Winning of the Initiative by the House of Commons," *Studies in History: British Academy Lectures* (edited by Lucy S. Sutherland, London).
NOXON, JAMES. 1973. *Hume's Philosophical Development: A Study of his Methods* (Oxford).
PALGRAVE. SIR FRANCIS. 1844. "Hume and his Influence Upon History." *Quart. Rev.* **73**: pp. 536-592.
PASSMORE, JOHN. 1968. *Hume's Intentions* (New York).
PEARDON, THOMAS, P. 1933. *The Transition in English Historical Writing, 1700-1830* (New York).

112 HISTORY OF ENGLAND

Pocock, J. G. A. 1951. "Robert Brady, 1627-1700. A Cambridge Historian of the Restoration." *Cambridge Hist. Jour.* **10**, 2: pp. 186-204.
———. 1967. *The Ancient Constitution and the Feudal Law: A Study of English Historical Thought in the Seventeenth Century* (New York).
———. 1971. *Politics, Language and Time: Essays on Political Thought and History* (New York).
———. 1975. *The Machiavellian Moment: Florentine Political Thought and the Atlantic Republican Tradition* (Princeton).
———. 1976. "Modes of Political and Historical Time in Early Eighteenth Century England." *Studies in Eighteenth-Century Culture* **5**: pp. 87-101.
Price, John Valdimir. 1965. *The Ironic Hume* (Austin, Texas).
Sabine, George. 1906. "Hume's Contribution to the Historical Method." *Philos. Rev.* **15**: pp. 17-38.
Smith, Norman Kemp. 1948. "Hume's Relations to His Calvinist Environment." *Dialogues Concerning Natural Religion*, pp. 1-8.
———. 1941. *The Philosophy of David Hume: A Critical Study of Its Origins and Central Doctrines* (London).
Stewart, John B. 1963. *The Moral and Political Philosophy of David Hume* (New York).
Stockton, Constant Noble. 1971. "Hume—Historian of the English Constitution." *Eighteenth-Century Studies* **4**, 3: 277-293.
Thompson, James Westfall. 1941. *A History of Historical Writing* (2 v., London).
Trevor-Roper, Hugh R. 1940. *Archbishop Laud* (Oxford).
———. 1963. "Hume as a Historian." *David Hume: A Symposium* (edited by D. F. Pears, London).
———. 1967. "The Scottish Enlightenment." *Studies on Voltaire and the Eighteenth Century* **53**: pp. 1635-1658.
Walton, Craig. 1976. "Hume and Jefferson on the Uses of History." *Hume: A Re-evaluation* (edited by Donald W. Livingston and James T. King, New York).
Wertz, S. K. 1975. "Hume, History and Human Nature." *Jour. the History of Ideas* **16**: pp. 481-496.
Willson, Davis Harris. 1967. *King James VI and I* (New York).
Wormald, B. H. G. 1964. *Clarendon: Politics, Historiography and Religion* (Cambridge).
Yule, George. 1958. *The Independents in the English Civil War* (Cambridge).

Index